Opens Like a Flower, Cut it with a Knife

A Buddhist mother's journey through grief

written by Cecilia Mitra

Published in 2020 by Fremantle Recording Studios.
email: books@fremantlerecordingstudios.com.au

Edited by: Shunit Jake Mitra
Cover graphic designer: Edwin Fong

ISBN: 978-0-6487415-1-0

Disclaimer

I am speaking purely from personal experience as a bereaved mother and as a Dhamma practitioner who had been meditating for many years before my son died. I am not giving professional advice to anyone.

This book is not intended as a substitute for the medical recommendations of medical physicians, mental health professionals and other health professionals.

This book is intended to offer information that will help you as a reader to co-operate with medical physicians, mental health professionals and other health professionals for optimum well-being.

Please seek the advice of a qualified professional before attempting to use any of the ideas presented in this book.

Do not make meditation a substitute for medication prescribed for you by your medical physician, mental health professional and other health professionals.

DEDICATION

To my beloved son.

CONTENTS

FOREWORD BY AJAHN BRAHM

There is much that I will never know. Such as the extreme inner agony that a mother feels after finding her thirty year old son, a part of who she is, laying dead at home. I cannot know what is too deeply personal for sharing.

This excellent book, nevertheless, took me closer to appreciating a fraction more of that pain. It was like being allowed a special place, outside in the garden, so that I could glimpse through a closed window into a house to see a dear friend, the mother, weeping without being able to cry. I cannot enter that house to offer help, it is not my house. But I feel a strange sense of gratitude to her for letting me look in. She let me read an early edition of this book.

Sometimes, we all need to know the dense darkness of despair, to feel it, embrace it and then be free - from inside out.

It helps enormously NOT to be a 'fault finder'. Trying to blame someone else always comes back to laying the blame on one-self. Instead, we take the way of understanding that tragedy is part of nature, so is joy part of nature. They are inseparable opposites. They go everywhere together, although one often lags behind.

Facing truth demands all of our courage. The path to freedom is the most frightening and may often seem too much. But we carry on. Life has no 'U-turns'. The quicker we get to realize, and accept, that the nature of this life is often capricious , the sooner we will walk out from the darkness of hopelessness into the fresh life of lightness and freedom.

SUFFERING IS, INDEED, ASKING FROM LIFE SOMETHING THAT IT CAN NEVER GIVE TO YOU. INSTEAD, MAKE PEACE, BE KIND AND LIVE GENTLY

INTRODUCTION

At some point in our lives, we will encounter a life-changing moment when we are forced to question our very existence. For me, it was when I found my thirty-year-old son, for no apparent reason, dead on his bed on an otherwise ordinary Monday morning.

I have written this book with the hope that it can help someone else through their own loss and grief.

The death of a child, at whatever age, is the most tragic experience for a parent, especially if the death is sudden. It's like a part of our body has been cruelly torn off.

We will never get over the death of our child, nor should we have to. Our lives will never be the same. We will think about our child every day for the rest of our lives, and we will continue with a background ache for our child. But I have found out that we can heal from the trauma and the excruciating pain, and we can even laugh again.

To heal well, we have to alter our views, our values, our attitudes, and our relationships. Expect that healing is a process which will take time.

The first step in the healing process was, for me, to learn to forgive and love myself for having outlived my beloved son and having gone against the expected order of things. It was not my doing, and it was not within my control. It's just life.

I had to accept that my son's death can never be undone. And I faced the painful truth that to be born is to die, and that life gave me no choice as to when, how or who died first.

Grief is devastatingly painful. It can either leave us with anger and bitterness or can be used as a new awareness to give a realistic perspective and meaning to our lives.

Viktor Frankl, in his book, *'Man's Search for Meaning'*,[1] wrote about his life as a Nazi concentration camp prisoner where he chose to transform his darkest despair into a search for meaning and he said,

> *'It did not really matter what we expected from life, but rather what life expected from us.'*

Our most difficult moments are our best teachers; for it is only when we encounter life-shattering moments, that we can see things as they truly are. But only if we become awakened by the tragedy and pick ourselves up - realising that *we ourselves must make the effort*[2] *to walk the path*[3].

---

[1] Man's Search for Meaning by Viktor Frankl, 1992 Edn.

[2] Dhammapada verse 276.

[3] The path meaning the Noble Eightfold Path - see The Dhammapada verse 275.

'Opens like a flower, cut it with a knife' is the title of a song written by my son, some five years before he died. I came across this song only after he died. When I examined the lyrics closely, I felt it was almost as if my son, knew that he would have a short life and had left me insights on how to deal with life without him through his song.

It helped me understand that although grief cuts deep like a knife and leaves a gaping hole in your heart, it is nonetheless, the very source from which a flower can bloom. It is only when you come to acceptance of your grief, that paradoxically, beautiful insights can arise. But this can only happen if we are prepared to delve deeper to investigate the meaning of it all - each for ourselves. This book records my journey and shares my insights with you.

I learned through the depths of sadness, that before you can know kindness at its deepest levels, you must first understand suffering in its darkest places.

Through my most difficult times, I understood the significance of the Triple Gem in my life - the Buddha[4] as the best physician; the *Dhamma*[5] as medicine; and the *Sangha*[6],

---

[4] The term Buddha means the awakened one. The historical Buddha, Siddhartha Gautama was born in the 5th century BCE in Lumbini (Nepal). He gained his enlightenment in Bodh Gaya, while meditating under a bodhi tree.

[5] Dhamma (Pali) or Dharma (Sanskrit) in this book mean the teachings of the Buddha.

[6] The Sangha as the third factor of the Triple Gem is defined as those attained to any of the Eight Stages of Enlightenment (the 4 usual stages divided into Path and Fruit)

as mentors for me not just to survive, but to emerge a better person. I only wish I could have gone through this journey without the death of my son, but this is the journey that has been thrust upon me, albeit not by choice.

Happiness and grief are part of human existence. Both joy and sorrow are inseparable, as beautifully expressed by Kahlil Gibran in his book, 'The Prophet'[7]:

> "Your joy is your sorrow unmasked and the
> selfsame well from which your laughter rises
> was oftentimes filled with your tears. And how
> else can it be? The deeper the sorrow carves into
> your being, the more joy you can contain'

and he said,

> 'When you are joyous, look deep into your heart
> and you shall find it is only that which has given
> you sorrow that is giving you joy.
> When you are sorrowful look again in your
> heart, and you shall see that in truth you are
> weeping for that which has been your delight...'

---

who are 'worthy of gifts, hospitality, offerings and reverential salutations, and who are the unsurpassed field of merit in the world' - The Meaning of Sangha by Ajahn B Brahmavamso (http://www.buddhistinformation.com).

[7] The Prophet by Kahlil Gibran.

CHAPTER 1

PEOPLE WATCH YOUR LOVE DIE

Rivers pouring down from the sky
Drowning all the people who did not
get to the high.

Although all of us have experienced suffering in some way or another, most of us will not truly comprehend the truth of suffering until we are confronted with a shattering tragedy that crushes our very foundation and forces us to question everything.

Here, I am not talking about the ordinary losses, but loss that is tragic and life-changing such as the loss of a loved one.

The loss of a child is one of the most tragic losses anyone

can experience. Nothing in life prepares us for it. We are not taught any coping skills for this. When my son died suddenly, I was stunned and paralysed with grief. It threw my life into utter hopelessness and chaos.

There are no words to adequately describe what sudden loss feels like. It makes you lose confidence in everything - your world as you knew it has now been utterly shattered: no chance is given to even say goodbye. Untimely, unexpected, sudden deaths leave many words unsaid and questions unanswered. Just shock and utter confusion. You need time to take in and process everything. And for many of us, sleeping is difficult, eating is difficult, just staying alive is difficult.

I received much advice from people who had not experienced the loss of a child. Although the advice given may have been well-meaning, I just wanted to hear from someone who had experienced the same loss I was facing.

In my wildest dreams, I did not imagine that on an apparently normal Monday morning, I would find my son dead on his bed. With no prior warning, no reason - just dead on his bed! All I could think of was 'Why? *How is this even possible? What is the meaning of this?*'

The deep, agonising emotional pain of grief made me physically sick. I felt a constant ache of my left shoulder and my stomach was in perpetual pain too. For a while it felt like

I was dying. The numbness, the anguish, the sadness, the pain. Oh! the incredible pain of body and mind that followed was unbearable. On some days, even breathing was difficult.

Although I had a lot of support from my loving family, relatives, monastics and friends, for which I was very grateful, what I desperately longed for was contact with other mothers who had also lost a child. Sadly, at first there was no such person I could talk to and I felt alone in my grief.

To make it harder, I was holding a leadership role and had responsibilities, not just personal, but for the Buddhist community.

As a Buddhist mother, I was conflicted. I believed I had understood the teachings of the Buddha - that life is suffering, attachment causes suffering, that all conditioned things are subject to death, but now I realised that it was mostly theoretical knowledge.

I was overwhelmed with pain that was unyielding - an intense unbearable pain, 'What should I do?'. I wished there had been a Buddhist mother who had experienced the same loss that I could have turned to.

In the words of Ajahn Chah[8], 'Theory and practice–the first *knows the name of a medicinal plant, and the second goes to find it and uses it*.

So, for me as a *Dhamma* practitioner of over twenty years, *walking the Noble Eightfold Path*[9] meant being able to apply the *teachings* at this most painful time in my life. To survive, I had no choice but to use the *Dhamma* as my raft to get up to higher ground lest I drown. It provided the tools, but I had to have the confidence to use it as medicine for my grief.

We have no choice at what life throws us, but we have what Viktor Frankl called, *'the last of the human freedoms, freedom to choose one's attitude in any given set of circumstances'.*[10]

When we choose the last of human freedoms - we can choose to be a survivor and not the victim of the circumstances.

About six months after my son's death, I was fortunate enough to meet some incredible mothers who shared their stories. A mother whose only child had been found dead in the park and who had to identify his body at the mortuary,

---

[8] https://en.wikipedia.org/wiki/Ajahn_Chah

[9] Right understanding, right intention, right speech, right action, right livelihood, right effort, right mindfulness and right concentration. This path leads to the end of suffering - see also The Dhammapada verse 277.

[10] Man's Search for Meaning at loc .905 of 2003

a mother whose teenage child was found hanging in his room, a mother whose son died of a work accident, a mother whose adult son died of a terminal illness, and a mother whose daughter went out dancing with friends to celebrate her twenty-first birthday and that same night died while dancing.

On hearing their stories, I was overwhelmed with compassion for these amazing women, and somehow my own grief became lighter.

I found I could even extend support to a mother whose only child had just died. Months later, she told me that I had really helped her at her darkest time because I understood how she felt. At that moment, I knew that I would survive my grief.

CHAPTER 2

UNRAVELLING, ABSOLUTELY EVERYTHING

Unravelling, absolutely everything
Slowly pouring down
I'm gonna let it all out now

Just like a great song, anyone who has gone through great loss has a story to tell. Telling one's story is primal in the grieving process, and you have to let it all out. The story must be shared and must be witnessed if healing is to take place at all. It bears witness to our unbearable loss and helps release our suffering, even as we re-live it. Our story gives meaning to the fact that our child has died, and it marks the start of the healing process.

For me, it all began on Monday, November 19th that fateful

year, when my life, as I knew it, ended!

At about 7am, just after breakfast, I walked to my son's accommodation unit located at the rear of our property just to check on him. The previous night he had not answered my call nor replied to my text message. I wanted him to know I had some food for him. It was not unusual of him to miss calls in the evening especially as he had just bought new DJ music equipment[11] and would have probably been trying them out with headphones on-so I thought!

On reaching his unit, I saw through the bathroom window that his bedroom light was still on. Occasionally he would be asleep with the light left on, so again I did not think much of it.

I knocked on the door of the unit which was locked, as it usually is, when he is home. There was no response. He usually responded. I started to feel uneasy and walked round to his bedroom window. I knocked three times calling his name. No answer. So, I then peered through a gap at the side of the closed blinds. He was lying on his bed, facing upwards, with the ceiling light illuminating his face. His eyes were half open and gazing downwards. There was something strange about how he looked, and I instantly feared that he was not asleep, but that he may be dead. *But how could it possibly be? I must be mistaken!*

---

[11] He just started as a DJ doing techno music.

Immediately I rushed to the house to get the keys and rushed back to my son's unit. I remember fumbling with the keys, opening the door and standing between the kitchen and his bedroom and at that very moment- I knew for certain he was not asleep - that he was dead!

It was a terrifying, dreadful, life-changing moment. It was so surreal, everything in slow motion as I tried to process what had just happened, and yet the first thing that gripped me was, *'how should I tell my husband?'* I felt that I needed to protect him from the devastating impact of this life-changing moment.

I walked back to the house and from the bottom of the staircase called out to my husband who was upstairs, *'I think there is something wrong with Brian'*. I tried to sound as calm as possible. At that moment my mind was brought back to forty-two years ago, when my uncle suffered a serious heart attack upon hearing that my father, his brother, had died.

Many questions were rushing through my mind, *'How do I tell my husband that our son is dead? How will he react? Will he get a heart attack?'*

My husband and I often say to each other that we are so blessed with three beautiful children who are also our best friends. Now I have to inform him that our son is dead!

On hearing me, he immediately rushed down and our youngest daughter who was downstairs, getting ready for work, had overheard. She too rushed out and together, we walked quickly to my son's unit. When we were half-way there, I said, *'I think Brian is dead'*.

Everything was like a dream and I cannot remember very much about what happened then. I just remember being really sad and crying and trying to process everything that had happened and also trying to remain strong. It was the most traumatic moment in my life and even writing this now, more than a year later, causes me deep sadness.

I called *000* - the operator stayed with me on the line until the ambulance arrived, which was in a few minutes.

Soon after that, I called the monastery[12] and remember the monk who answered the phone asked: *'Cecilia are you okay?'* My reply was: *'I am not okay.'*

I had confidence in Ajahn Brahm[13], who would have received similar distressed calls like this, in his over forty years as a senior Buddhist monk. He returned my call a few minutes later, and I told him that I found my son dead on his bed, *'I don't know why or how this happened. What should I do?'*

---

[12] Bodhinyana monastery in Serpentine, Western Australia

[13] https://en.wikipedia.org/wiki/Ajahn_Brahm

Ajahn Brahm said some comforting words and advised me to ensure that the family look out for and take care of each other at this most difficult time.

That morning everything was so bizarre. I felt that I had to continue to protect my family. I was almost robotic. I felt I had duties to perform. It was as if my ship was sinking and I had to ensure that everyone was brought to safety. I told myself I had to be calm for the family, especially for my son.

I told myself that I should not think about myself; it was my duty to guide my son through these tragic circumstances. I felt that he could hear us, and I did not want him to feel sad or guilty that he was leaving us in distress. I felt it was my duty, as his mother, to do everything necessary for the best re-birth possible for him. I wanted him to know that it was all right for him to leave us and move on to his next life.

It was like my years of meditation and learning the *Dhamma* were guiding me at this earth-shattering moment. This was, I felt, the last thing I could do for my child–*the worst has happened and now he needs to move on to his next life.* I also remember telling myself, '*I must not think of myself, I have to be strong for my child.*'

Often in movies, in the scene in which a woman is informed that her child has died, she falls apart and faints. I always assumed that I too would faint or fall apart if I ever found my child dead. But I have come to understand that most of

29

us are stronger than we realise.

I kept asking myself, 'W*hy?'* and '*How did this happen?'
How can something like this even happen?* A sudden death
takes your mind to the darkest places possible. Many
thoughts arose in my mind as to the circumstances and
cause of death, '*Was it suicide? were drugs involved?'*

It was like I was in an old black and white movie running in
slow-motion. I was in the cast and was the viewer at the
same time. Except that I couldn't turn off the set. And my
life was changing right before my eyes. My beautiful son
was dead on his bed and no one knew why. To my horror,
the movie was going on and on and there was no stop
button.

Later that morning, we were told by the police that their
investigations showed that the probable cause of death was
concussion from a fall in the bathroom. They deduced that
afflicted with diarrhoea and vomiting, he had slipped while
existing the shower, hitting the side of his head, thereby
losing consciousness for a while in the bathroom, before
returning to bed where he then died in his sleep.

Meanwhile, our youngest daughter called our older
daughter, who was driving to work. She did not tell her
sister why but asked her to come immediately. Our older
daughter knew from the tone of her sister's voice that
something serious had happened. We also informed our

closest relatives, and they came over immediately that morning.

The police were around for a while and when they had finished, the four of us sat with my son, held him and spoke gently to him and read the *Metta Sutta*[14] to him.

Then the people came to wheel my son away. As he was being wheeled out, I walked with him and with all my might, I tried very hard to refrain from crying and just kept repeating like a mantra, *'Brian may you have the best re-birth possible, may you have the best re-birth possible, may you have the best re-birth possible'*. I had to ensure that he went away with as little sadness as could be and that he did not have to worry about us.

The next day, we went to the mortuary to see him. Already he was different. To me, it was just a cold empty body that used to house my son. I would expect that any mother on first touching the cold body of her child in the mortuary would ask this same question. *'Where has my beloved child gone?'*

We were later told by his dear friend, that on the Sunday morning i.e. the day before he was found dead, he had called her because he was having an 'anxiety attack'. She would always help calm him when he had his 'anxiety

---

[14] *Metta Sutta* is the Buddha's words on loving kindness.

attacks'. No one would have thought anything more of it as Brian had been told by his doctor that his symptoms were of anxiety.

But Later in the week, we were informed by the Coroner's office that it was his heart that had stopped and that he did not die of concussion as thought. We had consequently to wait for a toxicology report to be prepared to determine why exactly his heart had stopped as this was unusual for a thirty-year-old.

A few weeks after the funeral, just before Christmas, we received a letter from the Coroner's office to advise that immediate family members should arrange to undergo medical checks of their hearts. It also informed us not to expect a final report until well into the next year.

It was like an eternity waiting for the toxicology report. Our lives were put on hold as we waited for the Coroner's findings - a long, unsettling time. To prepare ourselves for whatever the Coroner might conclude we had to explore every imaginable possibility of what might have happened.

We knew our son had been happy in the days before he died. He had been looking forward to releasing his music in Germany. So, we felt certain it simply could not have been suicide. However, over the long seven months, while waiting for the toxicology report, we had to grapple with the fact that many young men had been committing suicide unexpectedly. And because he had written some dark songs about suffering and life, we had to be open to that possibility.

During those difficult months while waiting for the toxicology report, we grappled with various possibilities as to the cause of his death. In the end, we came to a resolution - it would not matter whatever the cause of death might be because we loved our child deeply and unconditionally.

After seven long months, the toxicology report finally arrived. It confirmed that there were no toxic substances in his body. This meant that his sudden death was neither suicide nor drug related. It was a natural death. The cause of death as determined was 'coronary atherosclerosis' or in lay terms - a heart attack.

From the Coroner's Report, the cause of his death was unravelled, and everything became quite obvious. The breathlessness and anxiety in the morning, feeling unwell, the vomiting and diarrhoea - these are all standard signs and symptoms of a heart attack. Based on his last conversation, with a friend in the late afternoon on the day of his death, Brian thought he was ill from the oysters he ate the previous night.

In retrospect, everything fell into place for us - but who would have expected an otherwise healthy thirty-year-old to have had a heart attack?

On hindsight, as my father suffered his first heart attack in his mid-thirties, and as Brian was not only a heavy smoker, he often kept very late nights and was sleep deprived. It now made sense that it was quite possible for a thirty-year-old person like Brian, to have died of a heart attack.

CHAPTER 3

MOTHER'S LOVE

Rivers pouring out of my eyes
Numbing all my sorrows down

Brian was my firstborn, and the bond between a mother and a firstborn is very strong.

He was an adorable child, always happy. He grew up to be a gentle, kind, sensitive and loving human being. He was never shy of showing his love and affection for me and would always kiss me when he saw me and give me a hug before he left. There was never an unkind or a rude word from him. Monday mornings were our mother and son time, where we would do grocery shopping and have lunch together.

From time to time, he would send me random messages just to say he loved me. It never occurred to me that in his thirtieth year, I would find him lying dead on his bed and that there would never be any more such messages from him.

Four years before he died, he had bought a sewing machine for his girlfriend. I was excited for them and I ran upstairs to get a collection of my favourite fabric to give her. As I rushed down the staircase with the large bag of fabric, I fell and hit the corner of the landing wall with a loud thud.

I was on the floor and could feel that I had dislodged my front tooth. My glasses were flung off my face. It was a bloody scene. My son was the first to come to my assistance and he was extremely distraught. He accidentally stood on my glasses and was visibly shaken. But somehow even in that moment I was worried for my son and wanted to protect him, and I said to him calmly, *'Brian even if I was dying, this is not the way to react'*.

The instinct to protect one's offspring runs through the veins of mothers. Even when injured, I was worried about my child's well-being and instinctively wanted to protect him.

Like most mothers, I always expected that I would die before my child. He was very close to me and I knew he would have been in great despair should I have died. Little did I know that he would die before me and I would be the first person to find him dead!

I have now realised why I was relatively calm and mindful, and why I did not fall apart when I found my son dead on his bed. Subconsciously, I must have recollected my words to him earlier, *'Brian even if I was dying, this is not the way to react'*. Now the table was turned, my son was dead, not me. As his mother, and trusted friend, I had to apply what I had told him. I had to as often been said, *'walk the talk'*. I instinctively felt he was listening and watching, and I could not disappoint him. I had to ensure that I remained calm and mindful for him to be at peace as he moved to his next life.

I recall the story of Mother as told by Hans Christian Anderson:

'Did you see Death go by with my... child?' asked the mother

'Yes,' said the blackthorn bush. *'But I shall not tell you which way he went unless you warm me against your heart—I am freezing to death; I am stiff with ice...*

The mother pressed the blackthorn bush against her heart to warm it, and the thorns stabbed so deep into her flesh that great drops of red blood flowed. So warm was the mother's heart that the blackthorn bush blossomed and put forth green leaves on that dark winter's night. And it told her the way to go.'[15]

---

[15] The Story of a Mother is a story by the Danish poet, travel writer, short story writer

This story highlights the incredible magnitude of a mother's love for her child. There is nothing she will not do to protect her child from harm.

When my child died, I felt that I violated the basic code of motherhood - I had failed to protect my child. That my child was dead while I was still live had defied the natural order. No mother loses a child without feeling that she had somehow failed as a parent.

After Brian's death, I would recite the *Metta Sutta*[16] before each meditation daily and would break down whenever I repeated the words: *'Even as a mother protects with her life... her child'.*[17]

Over time, with meditation and reading the suttas again and again, I understood the truth of impermanence - that death is inevitable and that our children can die before us. The more we reject this truth the more we suffer. This brings me to the story of Kisa Gotami[18] at the time of the Buddha.

---

and novelist Hans Christian Andersen (1805-1875). The tale was first published December 1847.

[16] *Metta Sutta* in English.

[17] see line 26 of the *Metta Sutta*

[18] "Kisagotami Theri" (Thig 10), translated from the Pali by Thanissaro Bhikkhu. *Access to Insight (BCBS Edition)*, 30 November 2013, http://www.accesstoinsight.org/tipitaka/kn/thig/thig.10.01.than.html

Kisa Gotami

Kisa Gotami was the wife of a wealthy man of Savatthi. She gave birth to a son. But the child died as soon as he could walk. Kisa Gotami had not known death before and when they came to remove the child's body, she refused to allow them to do so, saying to herself that she would get medicine for her son.

Placing her dead son on her hip, she went from house to house, pleading for a cure. Everyone told her that she was behaving completely mad. Kisa, however, with her son on her hip continued to try to find someone with the right medicine for her son. She finally came across a wise old man who felt sorry for her and told her he knew someone who might be able to help. He directed her to the Buddha.

When she went to the Buddha, she said *'Venerable sir, is it true that you know a cure for my son?'*

The Buddha said that in order to help her, he would need special mustard seeds. And he asked her to find and bring back mustard seeds from any special household in which no son, daughter, or any other person or relative had ever died.

She thought it would be an easy task to find such a household and with her dead son on her hip, she immediately went from house to house in search of the special mustard seeds. But to her disappointment, she could

39

not find a single household that had not suffered the death of a family member.

Finally, the realisation struck her that there is no household free from death. It was a reality that she had to accept. She finally understood that death is inevitable and lay her son's body down and buried him. She then returned to the Buddha and asked him to teach her. The story goes on that she eventually became an *arahant*[19].

Another actual event from the Buddhist scriptures is the poem about the tragic loss suffered by Patacara who lived at the time of the Buddha. This had helped to comfort and soothe me in my grief greatly. The story goes that Patacara through a series of tragic accidents, lost her husband, her two sons, her parents and her brother. She was scorned as she wondered naked and destitute in her grief-stricken madness. Fortunately, she met the Buddha who showed her kindness. She heard his teaching, joined the order of nuns, and subsequently became enlightened[20]. Patacara later helped many other women overcome their grief, regain their sanity, and quench the pain of their loss.

---

[19] *Arahant* means a fully Enlightened Person.

[20] Enlightened means awakened. A person who is enlightened is also called an Arahant.

Pañcasata Patacara: verses of the senior nuns[21]

> 'He whose path you do not know,
> not whence he came nor where he went;
> though he came from who knows where,
> you mourn that being, crying, 'Oh my son!'
> But one whose path you do know,
> whence they came or where they went;
> that one you do not lament—
> such is the nature of living creatures.
> Unasked he came,
> he left without leave.
> He must have come from somewhere,
> and stayed who knows how many days.
> He left from here by one road,
> he will go from there by another.
> Departing with the form of a human,
> he will go on transmigrating.
> As he came, so he went:
> why cry over that?'
> 'Oh! For you have plucked the dart from me,
> so hard to see, hidden in the heart.
> You've swept away the grief for my son,
> in which I once was mired.

---

[21] 6.1. Paṭācārā, Who Had a Following of Five Hundred - see suttacentral.net Thig 5.10, Thig 5.11, Thig 5.12, Thig 6.1. It was thus that Paṭācārā, who had a following of five hundred, declared her enlightenment.

Today I've plucked the dart.
I'm hungerless, extinguished.
I go for refuge to that sage, the Buddha,
to his teaching, and to the Sangha.' [22]

The poem reveals that the Buddha, the Dhamma and the Sangha can provide comfort and refuge at our most destitute, and grief-stricken times.

---

[22] see also " Kisagotami Theri" (Thig 10), translated from the Pali by Thanissaro Bhikkhu. *Access to Insight (BCBS Edition)*, 30 November 2013, http://www.accesstoinsight.org/tipitaka/kn/thig/thig.10.01.than.html.

CHAPTER 4

CIRCLING THROUGH THE
EMOTIONS OF GRIEF

I experienced cycles rather than stages of grief. Elisabeth Kubler-Ross, 'On Death and Dying', described five stages of grief which I found useful - Denial, Anger, Bargaining, Depression and Acceptance[23]. However, I experienced an additional stage which was Anxiety. So, for me there were six emotions in my cycles of grief.

These were not lineal but rather more like circles because they would go round and round and repeat themselves. I spiralled through these cycles sometimes upward and sometimes downward and then start again. They were not predictable. They would come and go as they pleased and not be in any fixed order - lasting from a few seconds to a

---

[23] Some authors have criticised this and argued that there are seven stages of grief.

few days. They would repeat themselves until finally one day, I felt mostly Acceptance.

Some of the trigger factors that initiated these cycles were a photo, a song, a flower, a scent, or a passing thought.

It is not a matter of getting over it as it is getting past it and moving forward.

Long after the acceptance stage, I even experienced gratitude[24] which I will discuss later in this chapter.

Denial

The denial phase for me was very strange. I was the first person to see my son's body and so could not deny that he was in fact dead. But somehow, I kept believing that he would walk through the kitchen door saying: '*Hi mum, what are you doing today*?' or hearing him reply, '*really good mum*'. Or even seeing his knowing smile. The denial phase of grieving was the most confusing time for me. It was like my mind understood that my child was dead, but my heart wanted to believe that he was still alive.

Other bereaved mothers have also told me that the hardest thing for them is realising and accepting they will never-ever hug their child or hear their voice again. One bereaved

---

[24] Gratitude is the feeling of thankfulness for the benefits others have conferred on us and the desire to express our thanks. See also
https://www.accesstoinsight.org/lib/authors/thanissaro/lessonsofgratitude.html

mother used to meet her son at the bus-stop every-day at 6pm after work. When he died, she could not bear stopping at the same bus stop. She had to change her route.

For the first few months after my son's death, on the way back from work, I would reach out for my phone to call him but only to realise that he is not here anymore.

And the most difficult question to answer in routine conversations was 'how many children do you have?'

Although this is a question that most people you meet for the first time would ask just as a matter of small talk, it was a very painful one for me.

I, like many other bereaved mothers, have resolved this question by including our deceased child as one of our children. This may be considered a sense of denial, but because our deceased child will always remain our child in our hearts it is I believe the right way to answer this question whenever it is asked. If I feel comfortable with the person asking, I may choose to elaborate, but it is not a painful question to answer anymore.

Anger (and guilt)
After denial, came anger.

From the Buddhist perspective, hatred is the root cause for anger and guilt. Guilt is anger for oneself. I have therefore categorised these two emotions together.

For many months to follow, I found myself angry. The anger would come and go. It was quite a strange feeling for me as I am not an angry person by nature. I usually look at the bright side of things. But I could not see anything bright or good following my son's death.

Anger for oneself manifests as guilt

For many months anger and guilt overwhelmed me. It arose from a feeling that I may have somehow been able to prevent his death. During the months awaiting the Coroner's Report, my guilt would swing like a pendulum from '*I did not care enough as a mother*' to '*I should have exercised more tough love*'. This was because my son was found dead without a clear reason and there was a lot of painful effort trying to work out what might have happened. Every possibility needed to be examined.

For a mother whose child dies of suicide, she may feel guilty that she should have cared more, should have spent more time with her child or ought to have given more of herself. For a mother whose child died of a drug overdose, it may be guilt because she gave too much, or should have given more tough love.

For most of us, it is difficult to believe that we have been good mothers, no matter what the cause of our child's death, as that would mean forgiving ourselves for being alive while our child is dead.

Following the Coroner's report, I was again filled with guilt and kept questioning myself, *'Why didn't I know he had a heart problem?'* I think most people, especially mothers grieve along the lines of *'could have, should have, would have.'*

The hardest person to forgive is oneself

I had to process the circumstances of my son's death over and over again. The sequence of events just kept replaying in my mind like a broken tape recorder going on replay again and again. I realised that until I could forgive myself, I could not move forward. It was only when I understood and accepted that I could not have prevented this death, that I forgave myself.

I was also angry with the doctors for not sending my son for heart tests, and for dismissing his early heart symptoms as anxiety attacks.

Angry with my son for not taking better care of himself.

Angry with him for abandoning me.

Just angry at the unexpected death of my beloved son. I kept repeating these questions in my mind, *'why has this happened to me and my family? Am I not a good person? Why me? Why my family?'* These questions continued until *my anger dissipated.*

It took an incredibly long time, but gradually I realised there was nothing I could have done because the problem ultimately lies with the nature of life itself.

One mother told me that she felt guilty that she did not answer her phone when her son called - he was found dead that afternoon.

Another mother felt guilty for not being at home when her teenage son was found hanging in his bedroom.

One mother felt guilty because she felt she had pushed him in his studies, and he was found dead in his apartment.

All the deaths mentioned above could not have been prevented, and it was not the fault of the mothers. As mothers, we may feel guilty that we are still alive, and our child is dead, so we find reasons to blame ourselves.

Anger began to naturally dissipate when I developed *metta* or loving kindness which began with directing loving kindness first towards myself.

The Buddha said,

> *'Hatred is never appeased by hatred. Hatred is appeased by love - and this is a law eternal.'*[25]

This reminds me of a well-known Buddhist story often told by Ajahn Brahm - the Story of the Anger-eating Demon

The story begins with a king leaving his palace. When he left, an anger-eating demon entered the palace. The palace guards treated the demon with hatred and contempt as they tried to get rid of it. Because the demon thrived on hatred, it only grew bigger and bigger, and more nasty as it received more hatred. Finally, the demon got so large that it occupied the entire palace.

The demon was out of control and the king had to be summoned back. The king was a wise king, and he knew just the right antidote for the demon. When the king came back to the palace, he showered the demon with so much loving kindness or *metta* that the anger-eating demon became smaller and smaller as it became deprived of anger which was its food. Until finally the demon disappeared completely.

Similarly, when I practiced loving kindness, directing it first to myself, my anger towards myself disappeared, and eventually my anger for everyone else also disappeared. Initially, when I looked in the mirror, I saw a very angry person, my lips were in an inverted smile state and I was unrecognisable. I felt sorry for the person in the mirror staring back at me and thought that my son would be

---

[25] The Dhammapada v 3

unhappy to see me like that. I started smiling at the person in the mirror out of compassion, and eventually after many months, the person in the mirror looking back at me looked softer and the reverse smile was gone. Compassion for myself, helped me become a less angry person. Eventually, I learned to forgive and love myself even though I was still alive, and my son was dead. I begin to acknowledge and accept that it was not my fault; and that it was no one's fault that my son was dead.

Bargaining

At various times, I found myself bargaining. I would replay the whole scene in my mind and try to rewind the clock to see at which point I could have saved him. I would wake up in the morning with the same vision and keep replaying the *'if only'*. I had then recounted the different ways my son's death could have been averted in the hope the tremendous pain in my mind, my heart and my physical body would disappear.

Depression

Here, when I speak of depression, I am not talking about clinical depression but the immense sadness, melancholy and gloom following the death of a child.

Following, and along with, anger and guilt came depression. Together with depression, came anxiety, and they would flip between one to the other.

Depression is a normal part of grief and to expect that I should be okay, was undue pressure on myself. It is normal to feel depressed after the death of your child. As a Buddhist, understanding that everything is impermanent is the key, I understood that the depression too would pass. I had to allow depression, as an unwelcome guest, to sit with me and allow myself the time to process my loss. I understood that this is a normal process.

Primal Suffering

During my depression stage, my visceral crying would happen every day in the shower and in the car when I felt safe that no one could hear me. I made primal sounds, sounds that I never knew I was capable of making. It was like the sound of a wounded wild animal howling in pain.

The sudden death of my son left me swinging on a pendulum from utter sadness to deep anxiety. One minute, I was thinking of the past and how this might have been avoided and the next, I would be extremely anxious and fearful that other bad things could or would happen and I would have no control over it.

The saddest part for me over the next year was to accept that I would never see my son again. This realisation brought unbearable sadness. It would be triggered at any time by all manner of things like music, birthdays or anniversaries.

We should allow depression to serve its purpose - to limit us from doing more than we can handle, to allow us to slow down and to isolate ourselves from people generally. Isolation allowed me to understand my feelings, my relationships and re-evaluate the really important things in life.

I realised that depression relates to the past, and anxiety with the future. Meditation was extremely important in my recovery from depression and anxiety. It was the doses of present-moment living, during meditation, that was required to heal me. Meditation was my only medication in my journey of bereavement.[26]

Anxiety

My son's death sudden death brought on a lot of anxiety for me.

I would wake up in the morning in fear that I may find someone else dead. That was a really frightening time for me.

I felt so anxious and would go into panic mode if I called any of my family members and they did not respond immediately.

I was over-protective especially over my youngest daughter.

---

[26] More of this in Chapter 12

There was no reason for me to be so anxious over her. But now, she had to inform me of all her whereabouts. When she went out with her friends at night, I could not sleep until she got home. I would call her several times at night to make sure she was all right even though she was in her twenties and a very responsible person.

It became too much for her, especially when she too was suffering from grief over her brother's sudden death. She needed to spend time with her friends, or just be alone. I soon realised that my fear was stifling her and also implanting unwarranted fear in her. It then became clear to me that all my anxiety was just useless energy. After-all my son was at home in his own bed when he suffered a heart attack and died. Tragedy can occur anywhere or anytime without anyone being able to avert it.

One bereaved mother, whose son died in a sudden death from an accident told me she went through the same phase of being over-protective of her other children. She too realised that it was because she was terrified of another loss.

It is understandable for many people to want to believe in a god or deity in these circumstances as you feel that perhaps only some external superpower will be able help you. In a way, it is difficult to be a Buddhist, as there is no "Higher Being" to help you prevent suffering. No invisible Deity to pray to, to ask for favours, and no 'safety-net' as such.

Buddhism, however, is based on causes and conditions or the principle of causality. That all things arise and exist because of causes (or conditions) and cease once those causes (or conditions) are removed. [27] As stated by the Buddha,[28]

> *'When this is, that is.*
> *From the arising of this comes the arising of*
> *that.*
> *When this isn't, that isn't.*
> *From the cessation of this comes the cessation*
> *of that.'[29]*

There is no one to praise or blame. Good or bad things happen because of conditions and because of *kamma*[30], past and present. This should not be confused with fatalism - the view that nothing can change and that our past *kamma* pre-determines everything. We *can* do positive acts and thus change our past *kamma*. So, it would be fair to say that we are conditioned rather than determined by our past *kamma*.

---

[27] https://en.wikipedia.org/wiki/Idappaccayatā

[28] Also see https://www.accesstoinsight.org/tipitaka/kn/ud/ud.1.03.than.html

[29] AN 10.92 : translated by Thanissaro Bhikkhu

[30] *Kamma* (in Pali) is the same as *Karma* (in Sanskrit)

Kamma

*Kamma m*eans action and refers specifically to intentional action, mental, verbal or bodily act.

The Buddha said:

> *'I say that intention is kamma, because having first intended one acts with body, speech or mind.'* [31]

Positive actions motivated by wisdom and compassion are good *kamma.* Negative actions motivated by hatred, greed and delusion are negative *kamma.* Our past *kamma* conditions our present situation.

I can understand why some people would find solace in the faith they will see their loved ones in heaven someday, exactly as they saw them last. In fact, once I was specifically asked by a bereaved mother how it made me feel to have the view that I will never see my son again? Many bereaved mothers feel that their child is in heaven waiting for them. My answer to the question was that my son at thirty was different from when he was an infant or a boy - so which Brian would be waiting for me in heaven?

Some bereaved parents even preserve their child's room for many years after their child's death in exactly the way it was on the day that child died. The idea of keeping your deceased child's room in exactly the same way as he or she

---

[31] A.111,415

died does not allow us to let go and move forward just as much as our child should be allowed to move forward to their next life without guilt.

A seven-old child's room would be completely different from a thirty-year-old's room. What about our other children? Would we want them to grow and mature each according to their own directions while insisting that our dead child be frozen as at the time of his or her death while everyone else they knew grows older and different? What we would be doing is making a ghost of our dead child in our minds.

I can understand that believing that our child is waiting for us in heaven is a comforting idea. I used to believe that too, until about twenty-five years ago when I came across a newspaper report that triggered a fundamental change of perspective. I was a very devout Catholic then, going to church three times a week. I was fifteen when my father died in church, and so church was a very special place for me. The news article was about a two-year-old boy who had been raped and murdered in a Malaysian hospital toilet. Although I was living in Singapore and had never met or knew this boy before, somehow his story had upset me greatly. I began to question my beliefs. I questioned why this should happen to an innocent child. Why would any super-natural being knowingly allow this to happen? It also questioned my belief in the heaven and hell concept. Where would this child be after death - heaven? Is that for eternity for his two years of life? What about his assailant, what if he repents just before he dies? What if the assailant was only in his teens? To me eternity is too long a time for a reward or a punishment - whether in heaven or in hell.

Buddhism teaches that there is no static place anywhere- because in reality, life is never still or static. Buddhists do not believe in a stagnant or permanent self or soul. Even in a lifetime, the child is not the same as the adolescent; the adolescent is not the same as the adult; they are neither the same nor different persons. We are changing all the time[32] and we are what we are because of causes and conditions.[33]

A large part of me died with my son and I am now in many ways a different person. If we look around and examine things deeply and carefully, we can see that life and the universe is always changing in and around us. So how is it possible that when a person dies, he or she remains the same and unchanged, when everything else in the universe carries on as it always has?

So while I do believe I will see my son again[34], I don't cling

---

[32] Please see the discussion on change or transitions at chapter 15 of this book.

[33] As Buddhists we accept the concept of *kamma* not as a religious dogma, but we accept it based on personal investigation about how things in the universe are. Neither do we accept as true anything anyone teaches, including what the Buddha may have taught, without careful personal investigation.

[34] Buddhists believe that our loved ones are sometimes reborn to the same families

to the unrealistic belief he will look and behave exactly as he was at the point of his death. So, as it is in all the fundamental questions about life, the truth, in Buddhism lies in the mysterious Middle Way[35], between the extremes of viewpoints found in the world[36] - between Eternalism[37] and Nihilism[38].

Life is just a series of births and deaths in the cycle of *samsara*[39]. Whilst our loved one may be reborn and possibly even into our own families, that reborn being will not be the same person as our child. How could it be when even in one life a person changes so much from baby to adolescence, to adulthood, to old age?

The greatest solace to me is that my son was such a beautiful human being. He was full of compassion, wisdom, and love. He had sowed good seeds in this life and will bring his good deeds to his next life. I have the confidence that he will have a great re-birth; that he will bring much love and joy to his next mother. I am sure that she will love him just as unconditionally as I have.

---

because of their attachments to their loved ones.

[35] https://suttacentral.net/sn12.15/en/sujato,

[36] https://www.budsas.org/ebud/whatbudbeliev/111.htm

[37] The belief in the permanent soul.

[38] Nihilism or the view that there is no life after death.

[39] The cycle of births and deaths: the continuous process of being born, growing old, suffering, and dying again and again.

Acceptance

From excruciating pain, my grief improved to becoming a continuous dull ache.

For me, it happened when I eventually reached the stage of mainly Acceptance. This occurs when we spiral upwards and stay mostly at the Acceptance stage i.e. when we accept the true nature of life. Through right understanding, we learn to change our perspectives to life.

Acceptance is not about getting over your child's death. It's about acknowledging the loss and learning how to move forward. Acceptance is not about liking the situation, but it's about understanding that your child is dead and there is nothing you can do to change it. It is about accepting that you will never hear your child's voice again or be able to hug your child. It's about moving from the '*why me*' to the '*what now*'.

Acceptance is also about realising it was your child's time to go and that you could not have prevented it. It is about realising that you have to continue your journey without your child because it's not yet your time to die.

Acceptance is about a new normal in your life. Many changes were required for my new normal. To me it is about one less person at the dining table, walking into my son's empty bedroom, it's about not calling my son on the way home from work, and getting used to lonely Monday morning grocery-shopping alone.

Acceptance is about finding peace in your new normal. We may begin to get glimpses of gratitude for the time we had with our child after getting past Acceptance. When we lose a loved one, we begin to deeply appreciate their value and significance in our lives. We fully appreciate all the time we had with our child. Then we realise that our relationships with all our other loved ones are also impermanent and we begin valuing everything we have much more than before. This is something that will only happen after we get through all the emotions of grief. We see things with a different set of eyes. There is therefore sweet fruit that can come from the most bitter of tragedies.

Gratitude and the Four Sublime Emotions

A considerable amount of time after the acceptance phase came the feeling of gratitude[40]- my gratitude for having thirty beautiful years with my son. At long last, I was feeling a positive and beautiful emotion.

The Buddha detailed the following four highest states of emotion. He referred to them as divine or heavenly abodes of the mind[41]:

---

[40] The Buddha said that gratitude is the mark of a good person (VIN. IV,55) - see A Guide to Buddhism A-Z by S. Dhammika 2008 at page 110.

[41] Also known as the *Four Brahma Viharas - The Four Sublime States*, Nyanaponika, *1980*.

- *Metta* which is unconditional love or altruistic kindness (loving kindness). It is the anti-dote for hatred.

- *Karuna* or compassion. Compassion here is not only for others but also for ourselves, in times of difficulties or misfortunes.

- *Mudita* is sympathetic joy. This is the feeling of happiness that arises when we see happiness in others. When our child dies, it is easy for us to feel depressed or unhappy when we see others rejoicing in their children's achievements. *Mudita* is the opposite. It is feeling happy for the happiness of others. Rejoicing together with others in their achievements or success instead of feeling sorry for ourselves. *Mudita* is therefore the opposite of discontentment or envy.

- *Upekkha* or equanimity. This is a quality of profound balance, gratitude and acceptance of things as they are. It is opposite of depression and anxiety.

The early stages of grief bring the opposite of these *Four Divine States of Emotion*. It is only after Acceptance, can we experience loving kindness, compassion, sympathetic joy and equanimity. But how can one develop these states of emotion? Well, it's not through mindfulness meditation *per se* but through affirmation, which can be done before present-moment mindfulness meditations.

The Buddha said in the *suttas*:

> *Here, monks, a disciple dwells pervading one direction with his heart filled with loving-kindness, likewise the second, the third, and the fourth directions: so above, below and around; he dwells pervading the entire world everywhere and equally with his heart filled with loving-kindness, abundant, grown great, measureless, free from enmity, and free from distress.*

> *Here, monks, a disciple dwells pervading one direction with his heart filled with compassion...,*

> *Here, monks, a disciple dwells pervading one direction with his heart filled with sympathetic joy...*

> *Here, monks, a disciple dwells pervading one direction with his heart filled with equanimity...'* [42]

When we experience something so traumatic as the death of a child, we will go through so many emotions. We may finally come to an acceptance and get some understanding as to the meaning of life by looking at the whole picture from the birth to the death of our child.

If we are willing to move forward, we can start to see the

---

[42] Digha Nikaya 13, The Four Sublime States: Contemplations on Love, Compassion, Sympathetic Joy and Equanimity", by Nyanaponika Thera. *Access to Insight (BCBS Edition)*, 30 November 2013,
http://www.accesstoinsight.org/lib/authors/nyanaponika/wheel006.html.

higher emotions or states of mind to gain freedom from the negative emotions. We can be liberated if we actively choose to develop these four divine states of mind rather than dwell in the negative emotions. To develop these Four Divine States, we must be prepared to change our perspectives and attitudes - when we can move from the *'why me?'* to *'why not me?'*

CHAPTER 5

WORLDLY WINDS OF CHANGE – ARE YOU READY?

Gain and loss, status and disgrace, praise and blame, pleasure and pain are the eight worldly conditions that our lives spin around[43]. They are the duality of existence or opposites that make up the fabric of our lives. We rotate between these states mostly unaware.

When we cling to gain, status, praise and pleasure and reject loss, disgrace, blame and pain, we cause suffering to ourselves. These states are impermanent, transient and perishable. Freedom comes when we neither cling to nor reject any of these states.

Most of us spend our whole lives in fear of loss, disgrace, blame, and pain. So, we plan, and we try to control our fears by hoping or praying that we and our loved ones will

---

[43] https://suttacentral.net/an8.5/en/sujato

be spared from these states. We live in a bubble of ignorance that revolves around hope and fear. Based on hope and fear we plan our future thinking we can control our lives.

I remember that day in 1987 at my doctor's office when the pregnancy test had a positive result. My life changed in that moment. I would now be a mother! It was a wonderful time of my life - I was a partner in a legal firm and in a happy marriage. I would have a first-born boy who would take on the family name.

My two daughters were born not long thereafter, and I became the mother of three beautiful children. They had grown up to be incredible people who I love and respect deeply. They were not just my children but over the years; they had become my truest and closest friends in good times and bad. My husband and I often sought practical advice from them as they from us. For many people, their children become their best friends.

I had hoped and prayed that these states, which I considered my happy bubble of life or *'living happily ever after'* would never burst. Fear caused me to worry about the happiness and well-being of my family, especially my three beautiful children. In my innocence, I always thought I could maintain that bubble if I worked hard enough, planned hard enough, did charitable work and led a good life.

Fast forward thirty years, when my son was in the prime of his life and was eagerly waiting to take his techno music to Germany. We were planning to travel together to Berlin the next year. His personal life was in a good place and he was happy. Then on that fateful Monday, with no warning or goodbye, I found him dead on his bed...

On that day, my bubble of *'living happily after'* not only burst but exploded! *What was the meaning of this?* The following passage explains the duality of pain and pleasure and how one cannot exist without the other.

> *'The world itself has pain and pleasure woven into it as night is woven together with day. If we resist this truth, we will inevitably suffer... When we open the heart through the gate of sorrow, we sense how pain and dissatisfaction are woven into the fabric of experience.'* [44]

My son's life and death have taught me that there is no such thing as *'living happily ever after'*. Life is about duality or opposite states of existence. Pleasure and pain, praise and blame, success and failure are just part of our existence. *The beautiful fragrant roses bloom on a bush of*

---

[44] https://jackkornfield.com/truth-about-suffering/

thorns - no thorns, no roses!

These opposite states of existence arise in every relationship, including that of parent and child. When a child is born, we feel happy and elated. For some cultures, giving birth to a son elevates your position in life and brings gain and status as in the story of *Kisa Gotami* [45]. She married into a wealthy family and when she gave birth to her son, it elevated her position in life. When her child died, she felt she had lost everything.

As with the other bereaved mothers I have met, when our child dies, the initial reaction is not only pain but loss as well as blame and disgrace. These feelings are not justified but they arise and cause terrible suffering.

Everything that is born must die, everything we gain will be lost when we die, praise can turn to blame, and status or fame can easily be turned to disgrace. They are temporary states and rotate. It's like light and dark, hot and cold, happiness and sorrow – that is the duality of existence. To expect anything else is to subject oneself to suffering.

As explained by Ajahn Chah:

> *'Our birth and death are just one thing. You can't have one without the other. It's a little funny to see*

---

[45] See Chapter 3 on the Kisa Gotami story.

how at a death people are so tearful and sad, and at a birth how happy and delighted. It's delusion. I think if you really want to cry, then it would be better to do so when someone is born. Cry at the root, for if there were no birth, there would be no death'.[46]

The Buddha taught that all these conditions are part of life and we should not get attached to any of them. Attachment to these conditions or opposition to these conditions will bring suffering. As explained by the Buddha in the following sutta[47].

'Gain and loss, fame and disgrace,
praise and blame, and pleasure and pain.
These qualities among people are impermanent,
transient and perishable.

A clever and mindful person knows these things.
seeing that they're perishable.
Desirable things don't disturb their mind,
nor are they repelled by the undesirable.
Both favouring and opposing
are cleared and ended, they are no more.
Knowing the stainless, sorrow-less state,
they understand rightly, going beyond rebirth'.[48]

---

[46] See No Ajahn Chah- Reflections on birth and death - www. handfuls leaves.org

[47] https://suttacentral.net/an8.6

When we expect favourable states to remain permanently and reject change, we prime ourselves for grief and lamentation. And as expressed by Ajahn Brahm:

> *'Suffering is asking from the world what it cannot give you'*

It is okay to be happy when good things happen - but understand the universe is about duality and nothing last forever, good, bad or neutral - it keeps changing.

---

[48] AN 8.6 see also Https:/accesstoinsight.org/Tipitaka/an/an08.006.than.html

CHAPTER 6

THIS IS IT, IS IT ALL OF IT?
IS IT JUST LIKE WE PLANNED?

There is nothing more humbling to a mother than the death of her child. For months following Brian's death, as I cried in the privacy of my room, I crumbled to the ground begging to understand: *Why my child, and not I, had died?*

I always thought I had control of most things, but I realised that that was just a form of arrogance. The death of a child reminds us of the fragility of human existence. We are reminded that we are vulnerable, and that we are delusional when we believe we have substantial control over our lives.

Many of us live as if we are never going to die and work too hard; we live not in the now but for the future, planning and projecting. We even live under the false assumption that we have control of when and how we will die.

We may assume that if we are kind and charitable and have no ill-will for others, bad things will not happen to us. I made plans for retirement, to grow old with our children and grandchildren around us. These assumptions came crashing when my thirty-year-old, seemingly healthy son, died without warning.

We cry because we have no control of when death visits our family and we become depressed because of the loss of our loved ones; we lose hope and we might even thereafter define ourselves by the death of a loved one. We may respond to the loss by becoming scarred and bitter, or it can be our opportunity to grow spiritually *because of, and not despite of our loss.*

To grow spiritually, we must be willing to look inward and accept that this is just part of our journey called life. Our loss can make us more compassionate and understanding of ourselves and of others.

In life everyone will lose something or other, our health, our memories, our loved ones and even ourselves. The small and the large losses along our lives end, when we will leave behind all things that are precious to us when we die.

Brian always carried a bag with him wherever he went. In it, he carried his possessions like his phone, his laptop, his passport, his wallet. When he died, he had to leave his precious bag behind. His guitars, his recording gear, his clothes, even his beautiful body, like an empty container, were all left behind.

This is the nature of impermanence and we have to come to terms with this raw reality. How we deal with loss is what makes the difference. The key to our own happiness is not what happens to us, but how we relate to our circumstances. We can be the victim of the loss, or the survivor of the very same loss.

Loss is extremely complex and recovery from loss involves conflicting emotions. Each loss is different. We cannot compare the loss of a child to the loss of a parent or a friend or a job or financial status. The loss of a child is the most devastating loss I can imagine.

Some people fear death so much that they avoid being around bereavement, cemeteries and funerals. Some people keep their fingers-crossed or look-away every time they pass a memorial of an accident site on the road in the hope that it won't happen to them or their loved ones, especially their children.

Unfortunately, death happens and often when least expected, even to our child. Life is fragile and unreliable. So, the best we can do is to live in the moment and expect nothing.

Whilst some may take the view that we have absolute

control of our lives, others may take the fatalistic view that everything is pre-determined, and we have absolutely no control of anything. That would mean that we might as well cross the street with our eyes closed and take no responsibility for our actions. That is not what the Buddha taught. The truth lies in the middle way and that is between absolute control of our destiny and no control whatsoever. We should make plans which may come to fruition, or not. And if things happen out of our control, we should not be terribly surprised.

CHAPTER 7

DON'T FORGET
TO PUT THE MAGIC IN

My daughters did their very best to ensure that both of us were well. They were the parents for those days that followed. They cooked and looked after us. For the first few nights, they slept in the room adjourning ours so that the family could be together. *'If Brian could die in his sleep, what about the rest of us?'*, we thought. We were anxious and felt that we needed to protect each other.

The four of us spent much time together by ourselves providing strength for each other. We initially restricted the company of others. It helped us very much to gain our inner strength.

Our extended family and our friends also offered much support. Some relatives and friends flew in from overseas for the funeral.

We knew that my son's best friends, whom he considered his second family were in terrible grief too, so we organised to meet them at Brian's recording studio the day after his death. We were comfort for them and them for us.

We received messages, cards, flowers and food from so many people. The messages on social media from his friends and colleagues in the music industry kept pouring in. There was even a two-hour tribute broadcast from a radio station.

My daughters organised the funeral arrangements and the musical tribute by his friends as part of a beautiful send off for Brian. We had to make it a very special occasion of his life by doing our best to *put the magic in* [49]. To make his thirty years meaningful, it was important to celebrate his life, rather than to mourn his death.

The Funeral Day
The final viewing was for two hours, then the coffin was brought home where we were able to have our personal goodbyes with Brian. We had informed the funeral director

---

[49] This was what Brian did in his relationships. He would always give of himself unselfishly to make that relationship special. He also wrote a song 'Put the Magic in'.

as to what we required, and he prepared everything with great detail, from where we should sit in the limousine, to the colour and the number of single-stemmed flowers and balloons. We requested for thirty flowers and thirty balloons to celebrate my son's thirty years of life.

His body was at home for the last time. We kissed him and said our personal final goodbyes, and then they sealed the coffin and carried him out from our home. It was a very sad time for us.

Then we went to the funeral hall for the final send off - he deserved a beautiful send-off.

The hall was filled with the large crowd spilling on to the grounds outside. It was the largest funeral I have attended. Brian had touched the hearts of so many people. Even though it was on a Tuesday afternoon, people took time away from work to say goodbye to him.

Looking at the number of messages and people at the funeral, one realises that in the end it's only kindness that matters.

Brian was an unselfish person who gave generously to everyone he met. It is not the quantity of years but the quality of life that matters. Although he had a short life, it was very meaningful as he touched the hearts of so many people.

My husband, my daughters, Brian's close friends and I delivered our eulogies. And some of his close friends also performed musical dedications to him.

Ajahn Brahm gave a *Dhamma* talk on why some people die young and the nature of life and impermanence. He used the analogy of a concert which was appropriate, as Brian was a musician and did perform in concerts. When a person dies, it's analogous to the concert being over. We have enjoyed the concert, but it has to end. We want it to continue on and on and we often ask for an encore, but it must end sooner or later, and we have to part. We leave the concert with a beautiful memory, having had the time of our lives.

The funeral felt like we were hosting a party to celebrate his life. I hugged and thanked people for coming for to share with us in the celebration of Brian's life.

After the funeral ceremony, we went back to the studio for the wake. There were more songs and celebration by his friends and musician buddies.

We released thirty balloons with everyone repeating *'Brian, may you have the best re-birth possible'*[50]. It was a good feeling to release him metaphorically watch him go higher

---

[50] This signified not holding him back but to allow his spirit to move forward to his next re-birth.

and higher. We had to put the *'magic in'* to celebrate his beautiful and meaningful thirty years of life.

Many people told me the funeral ceremony was beautiful and I am sure that my son would have been smiling.

After the Funeral

People told me that everything would be worse after the funeral. They were correct. The reality hit home that my son was gone forever immediately after the funeral.

I recall a similar situation arising from the death of my father. The suffering was at its worst just after the funeral when we realised that my father was never coming back.

I felt that as Brian's mother, I still had to maintain my strength and not breakdown, as I thought he would hear me, and it would make him sad.

For the days and weeks that followed the funeral, as a Buddhist mother, I was concerned whether we did everything necessary to help him for the best re-birth possible. *Was he around, what should we say, could he hear us?* For weeks that followed, we tried to be mindful to prepare him for the best re-birth. I felt that as his mother, it was my responsibility not to do anything that would upset or disappoint him, as that may affect his next existence.

Many people have experienced a death in their own family.

But every relationship is different. Losing a parent or grandparent or sibling is not the same as losing a child. To me, as difficult as it was to lose my father at the mere age of fifteen, there was no greater pain than the death of my son. It was not in the natural order of things. In losing my son, I not only lost my beloved child but also my true friend, my future, my dreams and even grandchildren from him.

CHAPTER 8

IF NOT NOW, THEN WHEN MUM?

My son could not understand why I was always working and postponing doing more of the things I loved. *'If not now, then when mum*?' were his exact words to me on several occasions I can remember.

My husband and I always talked about getting a motorhome to travel around Australia. It was something we were planning for our retirement. My son's words, *'if not now, then when mum?'* [51] prompted us to get that motorhome for the journey round Australia about six months after he passed away, without waiting for retirement. If you wait till you retire, it may never happen. We now travel in it whenever we can for space and solitude in the great Australian outdoors.

---

[51] These words are Brian's legacy to us. It is a reminder of the impermanence of life - to make the most of each precious moment of our human lives.

Our Spiritual Journey

But at a deeper level, *'If not now, then when*?' - applies to our spiritual journey. It's about realising that if there's any possibility for enlightenment, the time is right now, not to be postponed to some future time. The future results from our actions now. It's right now that we are sowing the seeds for the future. Good seeds, good re-birth. Bad seeds, an unfortunate re-birth. There is no better time to apply the Buddha's teachings in everything we do than right now.

We are all going to die at some point - we don't know when. It could be the next minute, next hour, next day, next month, next year or even a hundred years from now. Walking into my son's room and finding him dead has made me understand that our time of death is utterly unpredictable and therefore it is up to us to make the most of each moment we live.

When we experience deep suffering, we may begin to understand the importance of Right View[52]. There can be something strangely noble, and paradoxically beneficial, about deep suffering when we realise that life is very dangerous and even treacherous. We can never get away from suffering no matter how much we plan or who we pray to. We should therefore never take the time we have left for granted but to invest it wisely to work our way out

---

[52] Right View or Right Understanding is the first factor of the Noble Eightfold Path. Understanding suffering and the cessation of suffering - the Four Noble Truths.

of the cycle of births and deaths.

'If not now, then when mum?' - sadly, it took my son's death for me to realise not only the deeply profound meaning of his words but also the depth of my son's wisdom. These words are a great inspiration to me to see things as they truly are. I reflect on them at the start of my daily meditations.

We may accumulate material possessions for gain, praise and status - continually expanding our little castles. This is like little boys and girls playing with their little sandcastles on a beach. As long as they are not free from craving for those sand castles, they treasure them, feel possessive of those sandcastles, yet when the sun sets and it's time to go home, they instantly abandon their formerly precious 'castles' and may even kick them behind knowing that the tide will sweep them away.[53]

Seeing anew

It is only when our child dies, that we will see some aspects of his or her personality that we overlooked or did not fully understand while he or she was alive.

For my child, from the time he was a toddler, he would carry a backpack everywhere. The backpack was usually empty. The backpack later, in his adulthood, was replaced

---

[53] https://suttacentral.net/sn23.2/en/sujato

by a satchel bag which contained his essential items. He would rarely be seen without his bag. The satchel bag was so much a part of his character that my husband and I felt it necessary to place it in his coffin. In retrospect, the empty bag, symbolises our only true possession which is our *kamma*.

When we die, we can take nothing, but our *kamma*. We are the heirs of our deeds that is our *kamma*[54] *as taught by the* Buddha. I knew that my son was a good human being, and so I was calm when he died because I knew that he had good *kamma*. He had nothing to fear, and neither did I, for his next life.

Intense suffering need not necessarily be an entirely bad thing because it can be an opportunity like none other to lead us to the path to wisdom. The path of wisdom is not to run away from the suffering but to understand the reason for the pain. This path is to be experienced moment by moment and is unchartered. It's like we cannot see where we are going, but only where we have been. Only we can walk the path ourselves, and if we do so without judgement or expectation, mindfully, one step at a time with compassion and wisdom like the two wings of a bird, we will eventually get there.

As expressed by Ajahn Brahm' *'If you want to be here, you'll*

---

[54] http://www.accesstoinsight.org/ptf/dhamma/sacca/sacca4/samma-ditthi/kamma.html

feel peace and freedom.'

CHAPTER 9

OPENS LIKE A FLOWER, CUT IT WITH A KNIFE

In March 1988, my obstetrician cut me with a surgical knife to deliver my son through a caesarean section. I was happy and overjoyed about the birth of my first-born child; the physical pain of the surgery was not suffering for me.

In Buddhism, there is a difference between physical pain and suffering.

Buddhism starts with the premise that life is suffering or *dukkha*[55] - which is known as the first noble truth. And what is the noble truth of suffering?

---

[55] *Pali* word for suffering

> *'Birth is suffering, ageing is suffering, death is suffering; sorrow, lamentation, pain, grief, & despair is suffering; association with the un-beloved is suffering; separation from the loved is suffering; not getting what we want is suffering.'*[56]

Most of us understand physical pain. It is the pain of physical injury and includes bodily pain of sickness, birth, old age, tiredness, and so on. Psychological pain is caused by our mental state and includes fear, worry, grief, lamentation, depression, anxiety and other negative psychological states.

In life, whilst we cannot escape physical pain, we can end psychological pain or suffering. When we speak of suffering, we are referring to mental or psychological pain.

Two types of Suffering
In this context, there are two kinds of suffering: the first, which leads to more suffering and second, which leads to the end of suffering. Ajahn Chah said,

> *'The first is the pain of grasping after fleeting pleasures and aversion for the unpleasant, the continued struggle of most people day after day. The second is the suffering which*

---

[56] Dhammacakkappavattana Sutta: Setting the Wheel of Dhamma in Motion (SN 56.11), translated from the Pali by Thanissaro Bhikkhu. *Access to Insight (BCBS Edition)*, 30 November 2013,
http://www.accesstoinsight.org/tipitaka/sn/sn56/sn56.011.than.html

comes when you allow yourself to feel fully the constant change of experience–pleasure, pain, joy, and anger– without fear or withdrawal. The suffering of our experience leads to inner fearlessness and peace'. [57]

The first suffering stems from ignorance, thinking that by feeding our desires; we will be happy. Feeding our desires only brings short term-happiness because we will soon be hoping for something else or be in fear of losing what we have gained. Greed, hatred and delusion fuel our desires. We are delusional when we think that we will never be separated from our loved ones. Fear of separation from what we love causes pain, grief and despair. Even when we get what we want, we suffer because of the fear that we may lose it. Hence these fleeting sources of happiness, from the Buddhist perspective may well and truly be called suffering and the seeds of suffering.

The second type of suffering is when we move towards the cause, rather than run away from it. In the case of grief, it is when we move towards grief rather than resist it. From a Buddhist point of view, this is the path to wisdom and liberation.

As Ajahn Brahm explains,

---

[57] *"No Ajahn Chah – Reflections", Complied by Dhamma Garden, 1994 see Chapter on Suffering 126/109*

> 'We should move toward our suffering with gentle determination. We need to listen to the prompting of our hearts and remain open like Patacara,[58] to a deeper understanding and a larger truth. That is what should always dictate our direction. We must resolve to move toward life, no matter how difficult or even perilous that choice may seem.'[59]

When we move towards grief, we begin to realise the truth that everyone and everything important to us will be separated from us at some point. It is the source of the latent or sub-conscious sadness that may be present even in our happiest moments. We recognise that nothing is dependable or reliable and our very existence is conditional.

Grief is suffering. It is the price we pay for love. When we love someone deeply, we will grieve deeply when we are separated. We love, and we have attachments to our children. When our child dies, we grieve. The more we love, the more intense the grief.

We also realise that it arises from attachment. Letting go of our attachments will release us and liberate us.

Whilst we may understand that our love for our children is born of our attachment to them, it's not good enough to

---

[58] Patacara who lost everyone she loved, her husband, her children and her parents all at the same time and went mad with grief. Yet she was able to understand the words of the Buddha and attained wisdom and enlightenment.

[59] Ajahn Brahm in Falling is Flying - the Dharma of Facing Adversity by Ajahn Brahm and Chan Master Guojun.

simply say, *'sever the attachment and your grief will be over'*. It does not work that way. This is an unskillful delivery of the Buddha's teachings and can be terribly unkind to a grieving mother. In her book, *It's OK That You're Not OK*, Meghan Devine published a journal by a grieving wife who said:

> *'I am angry with a Buddhist priest I desperately consulted early on to make myself more 'mindful' in my grief. He told me about the Four Noble Truths - that my suffering is all in the mind, and that I needed to let go of my attachment. Those were the cruelest words I ever could hear. He kept saying 'it's all in the mind, it's all in the mind.'*

The Buddha understood Kisa Gotami's grief. He did not ask her to *'sever her attachment'* to her child. But rather the Buddha taught her with compassion and wisdom and she was able to discover for herself that death happens to every family, as she walked from household to household and found no household free from death. When she was ripe with understanding, she on her own accord laid down her son to be buried.

Just like how the Buddha taught Kisa Gotami, everything needs to be nurtured gently and compassionately. Everyone is different, and we should be allowed to express our grief differently. There is a middle way as taught by the Buddha to Kisa Gotami, the way of compassion and wisdom, to overcome grief. We have to exercise kindness and allow ourselves to grieve without guilt. It is the quickest way to dispel grief.

The more we try to control our lives, the more we experience suffering. Trying to put a stop to intense grief is a form of control. Instead of trying to control, we should learn to practice letting go of attachments.

In the grief process, we have to be gentle. We have to allow the grief to pass; by observing its coming and going without judgment or control. Grief has a natural course and has to be allowed to be expressed, not suppressed. So, as part of learning to let go, we should also let go of our attempts to control the intense grief of the death of our child.

Unacknowledged grief does not make it go away; it just postpones the grief. It just makes the suffering worse. Suffering happens when we are made to feel guilty about our grief. Suffering happens when we blame ourselves for having out-lived our child. Suffering happens when we replay the events in our minds, like a broken record player, hoping for a different result. Suffering happens when we feel that we need to punish ourselves by being miserable and feel that we should deprive ourselves of joy.

We need to sit with the grief, like a good friend and observe it without judgment or guilt and allow the grief to naturally take its course. If we allow grief to leave, and allow compassion to visit, we may even open like a flower. Then when we are ready, gently cut that metaphorical flower open and investigate the source of grief like a skilled physician would for a physical illness.

If it requires surgery, the physician will cut it with a knife to investigate the root of the problem. Similarly, like that skilled physician, to heal well from grief, we should dissect and gently investigate the root of the grief. In the process, we will gain wisdom and understanding.

Letting go will naturally happen as we meditate. Meditation was my medication in the grief process. The more I meditated, the more I learnt to let go. Meditation is not about asking for favours. In other words, when we meditate not with desire, but with letting go, our grief will eventually become lighter. But again, this has to be done gently and with kindness to ourselves.

CHAPTER 10

WE ARE NOT ALONE

Although I was surrounded by family, relatives and friends, grief was a very lonely place. For me, solitude was required to move forward. I needed to understand what was happening. Everything happened so quickly. My life had changed in an instant and I needed the time-out to process this by myself before I was ready to let anyone in.

For months after my son died, even in a crowded room, I felt lonely and alone. I was no longer the same person. I was thinking differently, speaking a different language which would have been foreign to people who had never lost a child. I saw the world differently and my child's death raised so many questions in my mind:

'Why was everyone concerned with unimportant things? Don't they realise that everyone they love will die? Don't they know they will lose everything they own? Don't they

understand that everything is uncertain? So, why are they carrying on as if nothing has changed?'

Grief cannot be shared

Grief is a very personal thing and cannot be shared. Just as we dream alone, we also grieve alone. The intensity of our grief depends on so many factors like our relationship with our child, the age of our child, the circumstances of the death and our own mental and physical health at the time.

People react to grief differently and may be at different stages of grief even if they are in the same family. Every relationship to the deceased person is unique. A father-son relationship differs from a mother-son. The relationship between siblings is again different.

Also, people grieve at different times. For example, a bereaved mother who does most of her sobbing in the morning and during the day, will find it difficult if her husband breaks down and sobs at night when she is exhausted and just wants to sleep.

Although I had a wonderful, understanding family to turn to, I did not want to share every detail of my grief with them for many reasons. Mostly, it was because I did not want them to worry about me. They were already having a difficult time dealing with their own grief and the last thing I wanted was to burden them further with mine.

The very thought of losing a child is chilling to most people, so don't expect them to be of much help even as they try to support you.

People who have never lost a child do not usually fully understand what a bereaved parent is going through. There were times when advice offered to me by those who had not faced the loss a child felt hollow and insensitive. It often reflected their own fear of losing a child. Or it would stem from a well- intentioned motivation but bereft of any understanding. Some spoke simply to be seen and heard. To watch someone else grieve is uncomfortable and awkward, so often people needed just to say something, *anything* just to break the tension of silence. There were times when I wished more people were brave and wise enough just to sit with me saying nothing.

There were times when advice from well-meaning people did not sit well with me. I could not, as a Buddhist, be appeased by words like *'God has a plan'* or *'God loves you and he works in mysterious ways'*. In some circumstances, it felt like their advice was to gain favours from their God to spare them. I nodded and smiled but was not quite in the conversation and was more of an observer than a participant in these conversations because I understood they were acting out of their own fears.

Bereavement was also a time when I saw people in a

different light. Whilst there were so many people who were genuinely supportive, there were some supposedly good friends who I felt avoided us. There were also some who made insensitive and unkind comments at our most vulnerable time. So be careful as to who you allow into your lives at this time, as it can affect your healing process.

Also remember to say 'no' when you feel uncomfortable. For example, feel free to turn down invitations if you are not ready because you may end up feeling worse. You should take steps to protect yourself as you try to heal from your wounds.

I was fortunate to have many good friends and these friendships have helped in my healing.

There are four Types of Good Friends

The Buddha gave advice on how to recognise Good Friends. There are four Types of Good Friends: The helper, the friend who endures in good times and in bad, the mentor and the compassionate friend.

And how do we recognise these four types of good friends?

> *The Buddha said that you can recognise a helper on four grounds: They guard you when you are negligent, guard your property, keep you safe in times of danger; and when something needs doing they are there to help you.*

He said that you can recognise a friend who endures in good times and bad: They tell you secrets, they keep your secrets, they don't abandon you in times of trouble and they even give their life for you.

He also said that you can recognise a friend who is a mentor: They keep you from doing bad, they support you in doing good, they teach you what you do not know, they explain the path to liberation.

And that you can recognise a friend who is compassionate: They don't delight in your misfortune, they delight in your good fortune, they keep others from criticising you, they encourage pride for you.[60]

My Furry Friend

I was also fortunate to have a loving dog, Marlow, who was a lifeline during my most difficult time. He would sit with me quietly, not judging but just with caring eyes showing me that he loved me. And never leaving me alone when I cried. In the initial stages, he would even sit with me throughout my meditation and tried to be as still as possible. I would often break-down to visceral crying during my meditation. There were few times when I found one of his paws placed on me as I was crying uncontrollably. Marlow was trying to comfort and calm me as best as he

---

[60] DN 31 The Buddha's advice to Sigalovada found on SuttaCentral.net

could. It is incredible how sensitive dogs are. Now, he leaves me to meditate by myself as he must have sensed that I am in a better place.

Other Bereaved Mothers

The only other people I felt I comfortable sharing my grief with were other bereaved mothers who had gone through the same loss. With other bereaved mothers, I was not alone. We all shared the loss of a child and we spoke the same language. We understood the pain of losing a child. I connected with grieving parents. There are many bereavement groups in many cities. I would recommend that bereaved parents connect with such organisations.

It is important to speak to as many people as possible who have suffered the same loss. It's just like learning how to surf from experienced surfers, or to learn to cook from experienced cooks. Of course, be discerning and observe how these bereaved parents are recovering from their loss. The best teachers are those who lead by example.

I joined a bereavement group, where every group member had lost a child or a sibling. It was an important part of my recovery process. Before joining the group, I felt like I was the only mother who had suffered the loss of a child. We look at people in our circles, and we see that most of them have intact families and for most it is the parents who die first. We question our beliefs and values; it is natural for us to question:

'Why me? Why did my child die before me?'

When I met other bereaved mothers at the bereavement group meetings, it put things into perspective - I certainly was not alone, very far from it. There are so many other people who have gone through the death of a child. Some have lost more than one child. It is, sadly, a common everyday occurrence to lose a child. I understood that it was no one's fault, not my child and not me. Death happens. Birth happens.

I understood that there is no good or bad in death; it is just part of life. When our child dies before us, we have no choice but to learn how to continue our journey without our child. The bereavement group also helped me to understand that the feelings I was going through were normal.

It is important to know that you are not alone and that others have gone through and have survived the loss. Many have come out of the tunnel of grief better people. At every group meeting, there are new bereaved parents. There is much understanding to be gained just by listening.

Also, I always come out of these meetings with more wisdom and compassion, knowing that each minute people are born, and people die. Knowing that this was just part of life and that there was nothing terribly unique about what I was going through helped me place things in the right perspective.

CHAPTER 11

THE FOUR DIVINE MESSENGERS

When my son died, I kept recalling and thinking about my father's death. I realised that the death of a loved one brings back all the major losses in your life.

My father died when I was only fifteen years old. It was also of a heart attack and a sudden death. He went to church for the second time that fateful day. It was the first time I recall that my father went to church twice on a Sunday. As the hymn *'Come down Lord my son is ill'* was being sung, my father collapsed and was rushed to the hospital. When I arrived at the hospital, I saw his clothes on the bench in the waiting room and the doctors pulling off their stethoscopes. Someone said: *'call the next of kin'*. It was surreal. A scene I will never forget.

The next day when his body arrived from the mortuary, I bent to kiss my father's forehead. I remember the harsh reality and shock that his forehead was cold as ice. I remember, as a child, I blamed myself for not saying goodbye when he left the house that day. I even blamed myself for not praying hard enough. What a weird notion, thinking that I could have in any way prevented his heart-attack. After forty-two years, I started grieving again for the loss of my father.

Then I grieved for my mother. My mother is alive, but she suffers from severe dementia and has lost all memory of her past, including that of her children. She cannot recognise her children anymore. She would ask me who I was whenever I visited her. My mother has gone back to diapers, is bedridden and has forgotten how to speak in English.

The Buddha declared that there are Four Divine Messengers visible in the world for all to see - *a sick person, a dead person, an old person, and a monastic.* He said these are four *divine messengers* because they warn us that life is suffering and offer good reason to seek refuge from the impending suffering we all must face at some point in our lives. The Buddha used the term 'divine' because even a creator god, if one exists, cannot put the message more clearly. Hence any sick person, dead person, old person or any renounced monastic may rightly be termed a 'Divine' Messenger.

I have not only seen these Four Divine Messengers, but my own son dead on his bed, my own mother frail, old and sick and yes, I have seen many monks and nuns living happy renounced lives.

Brian's words: *'If not now? Then when mum?'* were ringing in my mind as I realised that my son, my father, my mother and the monastics were indeed Divine Messengers. The Buddha also spoke about the parable of the Four Types of Horses.

The Four Types of Horses

In the sutta, the Buddha taught that there are four kinds of horses.

> *The first kind is most sharp-witted, startled when it sees the mere shadow of the whip, and understands what the rider wants.*
>
> *The second kind is startled when the whip touches its hair.*
>
> *The third kind is startled only when the whip touches its flesh.*
>
> *The fourth kind of horse only behaves when the whip has penetrated to the bone.*
>
> *Then the Buddha explained that the first horse is like the person who realises impermanence when he hears that someone in another village died;*

The second horse is like the person who sees impermanence when he hears that someone in his village died;

The third horse is like the person who realises impermanence when his parent dies;

The fourth horse is like a person who doesn't realise impermanence until he faces his own death.[61]

If I were to ignore the Divine Messengers, I would be worse than the fourth horse.

The sudden deaths of my father and my son, although forty-two years apart have given me a greater understanding and insight that life is fraught with danger and can end at any moment, even in mid-sentence.

We have read so many times about the sudden deaths of others, through bombings and killings, accidents, plane crashes; but until sudden death happens to us personally, to our families, most are unable to accept or truly take impermanence as a reality.

When we face the truth of impermanence, we also will understand that it is greed, hatred and delusion that fuels the fires of the six sensual delights i.e. sight, sound, taste,

---

[61] Patoda Sutta: The Goad-stick translated from Pali by Thanissaro Bhikkhu AN 4.113. see also suttacentral.net: Bhante Sujato

touch, smell and intellect, from one life to the next within *Samsara or* the cycles of birth and re-birth.

If we choose to accept the 'message' from the Four Divine Messengers, we can ripen to see that all is burning and become disenchanted. The Buddha taught that we can be liberated from suffering through detachment and disenchantment from sensual delights.[62]

---

[62] 'The All is aflame. Which All is aflame? The eye is aflame. Forms are aflame. Eye-consciousness is aflame. Eye-contact is aflame. And whatever there is that arises in dependence on eye-contact, experienced as pleasure, pain, or neither pleasure nor pain, that too is aflame. Aflame with what? Aflame with the fire of passion, the fire of aversion, the fire of delusion. Aflame, I tell you, with birth, ageing, & death, with sorrows, lamentations, pains, distresses, & despairs.

'The ear is aflame. Sounds are aflame....
'The nose is aflame. Aromas are aflame....
'The tongue is aflame. Flavours are aflame....
'The body is aflame. Tactile sensations are aflame.... 'The intellect is aflame. Ideas are aflame. Intellect-consciousness is aflame. Intellect-contact is aflame. And whatever there is that arises in dependence on intellect-contact, experienced as pleasure, pain or neither pleasure nor pain, that too is aflame. Aflame with what? Aflame with the fire of passion, the fire of aversion, the fire of delusion. Aflame, I tell you, with birth, ageing, & death, with sorrows, lamentations, pains, distresses, & despairs. SN 35:28
 see https://www.accesstoinsight.org/lib/authors/thanissaro/likefire.pdf

CHAPTER 12

MEDITATION WAS MY MEDICATION

Words of comfort from others could not alleviate my grief. I wondered how they could they possibly know what I was going through? *Have they lost a child?* I just wanted my son back! But how's that possible? Even the Buddha could not bring Kisa Gotami's son back.

The only thing that helped me was meditation. I was in so much suffering. I felt that meditation was the only thing that could help me. I needed meditation as my medication to just be quiet in the moment, to calm my mind and to understand the intense suffering I was going through.

Flashbacks
I was having flashbacks of my son lying dead on the bed and some people were concerned about me. I thought to

myself;

'Of course, I had flashbacks - after all, I had just found my son dead on his bed!'

I felt It would have been unnatural *not* to be processing deeply and replaying the shocking scene I had just witnessed. For me, this was necessary for my healing.

The flashbacks were metaphorically, in retrospect, like the flashes from a lighthouse, which serve as a warning to ships of danger, and in this case, the danger of navigating through the ocean of *Samsara*. I was not sick, neither physically nor mentally. I was grieving my son's death and instead of numbing my pain, I intuitively wanted to gain understanding of my intense grief.

As an experienced *Dhamma* practitioner, this was the time for me to observe the intense pain and to investigate the causes. I personally did not need to be fixed by a pill. I was confident the *Dhamma* had all the tools I needed, and mindfulness meditation would be the method. I just had to be brave enough to sit through it; to heal my wounds.

As succinctly stated by Pema Chodron in her book, 'When Things Fall Apart,

> 'The dharma can heal our wounds, our very ancient wounds *that come not from original sin but from a*

misunderstanding so old that we can no longer see it.'[63]

The Buddha stated:

'The stream of tears that you have shed through countless lives in samsara, through meeting misfortune, is more than all the waters in the oceans.'[64]

Most people are generally afraid of grief and being around grieving people. They want all suffering and sadness to magically disappear with a pill. But grief is not something to suppress or to run away from. Life is suffering and running away from the fact of suffering only postpones our understanding of life. Intense suffering offers a unique opportunity, if we are not afraid to cut it open, to discover the primal source of the suffering. Once the source is exposed, the healing happens, completely naturally.

Buddhism is not just a religion or a philosophy, but a psychology that diagnoses and treats the ailing mind. It is not about trying to numb the pain but to move towards the direction of the pain and allowing the underlying causes of the suffering to reveal themselves. To the Buddhist, this

---

[63] When Things Fall Apart- heart advice for difficult times, by Pema Chodron.

[64] (SN 15.3). see also
https://www.accesstoinsight.org/tipitaka/sn/sn15/sn15.003.than.html

process of revelation, this investigation, this seeking, this allegiance to the truth, is the essence of what it is all about.

Meditation gave me clarity of mind. It made me more relaxed and released the tension when my body was stiff with pain. It gave me the freedom of not clinging to any identity, not even the persona of a grieving mother. Experiencing this freedom, even for a few moments helped me tremendously. I found Ajahn Brahm's book *Mindfulness, Bliss and Beyond*[65] helpful as my instruction manual and the book guided me through my most difficult moments in meditation.

Meditation is not contemplation
Mindfulness meditation is the opposite of contemplation. Meditation is letting go of attachments. Letting go of thinking, planning and contemplating.

Neither is it prayer or the asking of favours. It is not about expecting anything. Meditation is about letting go of the past and the future and just being in the present moment. It allows us to put down our burdens, however heavy. Over time, insights will naturally arise.

Meditation was my medication and I used it as my personal daily prescription. It calmed me first thing in the morning and helped me carry on. I would often feel sad or break-

---

[65] Mindfulness, Bliss and Beyond. A Meditator's Handbook

down again a few hours after meditation and needed to meditate again. I needed periodic doses of just being in the present moment, where there was no guilt or sadness from regrets, from the past, or fear about the future.

We perpetually carry around with us two metaphorical bags, one containing our past and the other our future. The past contains regrets and sadness and the future contains fears, worries and fantasies. We are always flipping through the contents of these bags - from past to future and future to past. Unless we are mindful, we are seldom ever able to lay down these two heavy bags.

I consider myself fortunate to have learned and practiced meditation long before my son died. So, when I needed it most, I was able to meditate even on the day my son died. It is a basic life skill everyone should develop.

Meditation three times a day was my personal prescription for the intense grief I was going through. It helped me to lay down the two bags of past and future. Just being in and with the moment was most important in my grief process – one painful, terrifying moment at a time.

I started each meditation reciting the *metta sutta* and in time, I learned to have loving kindness for myself. Through this process, a forgiveness developed within myself; I forgave myself for being unable to protect my child from death.

In the words of Ajahn Chah:

> *'Unless one has deeply wept, one has not yet begun to meditate'.*[66]

When you meditate focusing on the breath – breathing in and breathing out - you come to a stage when you begin to observe the pauses in the breath. Just as in meditation, pauses are important in everything we do. Letting go naturally happens when we learn to silently observe. The more I meditated, the more I learnt to be mindful in observing the pauses in my grief.

Then will come a time when there are more pauses than grief, but you must allow the pauses to happen naturally. When there are more periods of pauses than grief, that is when we know we are on the road to recovery. But again, this has to be done gently and with loving kindness for ourselves. When my mind became more peaceful, I began to find some answers to my questions.

---

[66] https://www.ajahnchah.org/pdf/no_ajahn_chah.pdf

A day without meditation was a day wasted
A day without meditation was a day wasted in my journey. For me, through meditation, insights would arise. Most of the time we live in delusion. It is only when we are hit with intense grief that we are ripe to question what the really important things in life are and we are willing to make those changes because life offers us no other viable choice. In the words of Thich Nhat Hanh:

'*No mud no lotus.*'[67]

I remember in the first few weeks after my child's death - I deeply yearned to understand the meaning of life. I questioned how something like this could even happen? How can one's life literally change overnight like this?

I hoped that some wisdom would arise through my meditations. Then quite suddenly and magically three words appeared on the screen of my mind: '*greed, hatred, and delusion*'. I understood that I had to ultimately end greed, hatred, and delusion to end all suffering. This is something we all know or acknowledge to some extent, but to understand it fully, one has to perhaps experience suffering at its deepest level.

Retreating from the world
Thankfully, about six months after my son's passing, I was

---

[67] No mud, No Lotus: The Art of Transforming Suffering by Thich Nhat Hanh.

able to join one of Ajahn Brahm's nine-day meditation retreats at Jhana Grove in Western Australia. It was important to spend time in the quiet, peaceful surroundings of a forest looking inwards for answers about life, death and why we are here. It was a difficult time with lots of tears during and in between meditations.

The retreat was like being in a hospital recovering from a distressing injury. Some things became clearer, and I got some understanding of the Three Marks of Existence. Even though I had heard all this before my son's death and knew the meaning of the words *anicca, anatta* and *dukkha,* it was all just at an intellectual level. However, as a mother seeing the whole cycle from gestation, then birth to the death of my son, the meaning of these universal truths became clearer to me. More about this in the next chapter.

I was grateful for the understanding but wished I could have understood this from some other way than through the death of my beloved son.

CHAPTER 13

THE THREE MARKS OF EXISTENCE

The recurring vision of my son's peaceful face lying dead on his bed was indelibly imprinted on my mind. The memory of his peaceful face would arise first thing every morning, every night before I slept and during my meditations. I thought the reason for my flashbacks was because I *had* to hold on to it, as I did not ever want to forget his face and did not want my memory to fade or come only from photos.

Discovering my son dead that morning was the saddest moment in my life, but it was at that moment I understood *dukkha,* the First Noble Truth that life is suffering.

Months later during the nine-day retreat with Ajahn Brahm, I realised the meaning and significance behind the flashbacks - his death had taught me not just the meaning of *dukkha* but also *anicca,* and *anatta.* These are the three marks of existence, an essential part of the teachings of the

Buddha. Finding my child's lifeless body with no prior notice or sign gave me a deeper- understanding of these three marks of existence.

Anicca: Impermanence

Anicca is a *Pali* word which means the absence of continuity or the absence of permanence.

> *'All things are impermanent*
> *when one observes this with insight,*
> *then one becomes detached from suffering;*
> *this is the path of purification'.*[68]

My son had been with us almost every day for thirty years, it was the natural expectation that we would continue to see him tomorrow, next week, next year. Never did I imagine that one morning, it would all be over. He would leave without a goodbye, a kiss, or a hug as he usually did. There was no warning whatsoever. We assume things will remain in an expected order.

We humans beings like to remain blind to the unfortunate aspects of reality. Change is a reality. If the change is good for us, we embrace it, but if it is an unfortunate change, we deny it or lament, *'Why me?'*

I suppose when we lose someone through old age or

---

[68] The Dhammapada 227 - Also see https://www.vridhamma.org/node/2489

sickness, *anicca* is not so obvious because the change is gradual, not sudden. With my child's sudden death - *impermanence* hit me like a ton of bricks. I realised that nothing is reliable or dependable. Understanding this profound teaching is understanding that we cannot depend on anything or anyone, not even ourselves.

Believing that things will always be constant brings immeasurable pain and suffering. When we accept *anicca*, we become more appreciative of everything and everyone because we realise that we cannot take anything for granted. We realise that there is no point being firmly attached to anything. Realising this, we can free ourselves from ill-will. No point holding on to negative emotions. Everything is impermanent.

Being cognisant of *anicca* is a liberation
This wonderful truth frees us and allows us to live positively and meaningfully. The Buddha advised sharing *these truths for the happiness and well-being of all.*

We cannot say we even own anything, not our material wealth, or our own bodies, as everything we supposedly own are impermanent and perishable.

The Buddha said to his monks:

> *'Bhikkhus, form is impermanent. What is*
> *impermanent is suffering. What is suffering is*

non-self. What is non-self should be seen as it really is with correct wisdom thus: 'This is not mine, this I am not, this is not myself.' Feeling is impermanent...Perception is impermanent...Volitional formations are impermanent... Consciousness is impermanent. What is impermanent is suffering. What is suffering is non-self. What is non-self should be seen as it really is with correct wisdom thus: 'This is not mine, this I am not, this is not myself.'

"Seeing thus ... He understands: '... there is no more for this state of being.'[69]

Anatta: No self

Anatta means there is no unchanging self[70].

I was the first person to see my son lying dead on his bed. When I saw his body, he looked calm and peaceful, like he was asleep. But somehow, I immediately sensed that he was dead. There was an unmistakable emptiness of the body. Although his scent was present, everything else had left his body. It was like a suddenly vacated home. The tenant's scent and his things were still there but it was an

---

[69] SN 22 see https://suttacentral.net/sn22.15/en/bodhi

[70] suttacentral.net - Identifying the five *khandhas* as 'self' is the cause of affliction SN 22.1

empty house, no longer a home. An analogy would be like when a hermit crab discards its shell, leaving just an empty shell. Similarly, when I saw Brian dead on the bed, I immediately perceived it as an empty body or container.

We own nothing, not our bodies, not even our breath. That's a very powerful teaching that my son taught me on his deathbed.

In Buddhism, we understand that we are essentially made-up of five basic parts – our body, our perceptions, feelings, volition and the six consciousnesses[71]. And in that instant, I grasped that he had very recently left the body.

This is not dissimilar to my mother who has severe dementia and who cannot remember anyone, even her children or who she is. People with severe dementia are like empty shells, and yet part of them is still present. It is proof that we are made up of different parts. In the case of Brian, everything but his body had vanished.

My mother is in her nineties but sometimes thinks she is in her forties. She has lost many of her senses. She is blind, is hard of hearing, almost fully bedridden and has almost lost her sense of taste as well. Lately, when she asked for chicken rice just after her lunch, and was given a cookie instead, she said *'this chicken rice is delicious'*. Clearly, her

---

[71] Contemplation of the six senses from MN 148 - suttacentral.net

taste awareness was absent.

Consciousness is something we like to think of as a singular core component of ourselves. Yet through my mother I could see that consciousness is itself made of six parts - taste consciousness, touch, sight, hearing, smell and mental consciousness.

From the death of my son and the dementia of my mother, I am now able to better understand some aspects of the Buddha's difficult-to-grasp teachings of *anatta*. We are not our bodies, not even our minds. Nothing exists by itself, all things are connected to other things.

Dukkha: Suffering

The Buddha had explained that attachment and clinging is the cause of suffering.

Following my son's death, I had a photo of him as my screen-saver on my phone, and placed his photos throughout the house, so that I could hold on to him and be reminded of him constantly. It is a common reaction of grieving parents to place pictures of their child everywhere as a reminder that they will never be forgotten.

I never allowed myself to rest from the fact that my son had died. For many months, there had been a constant pain of my left shoulder. I did not allow myself time to take a pause in my grief. Months later during the nine-day meditation retreat, quite unexpectedly, an insight arose, and I realised I had to change the screen-saver image of my phone. Like many people, I use my phone for everything, including checking the time, my alarm, keeping in touch with everyone. Hence the phone screen photo of my son was often the first and last image I saw each day. I saw it whenever i picked up the phone during the day, and so it acted as a constant reminder of my bereavement.

As soon as I replaced the photo, the pain in my left shoulder vanished. I was amazed. I suppose the image had been a constant reminder that I was or ought to be in perpetual grief. I still have lots of photos of my son on my phone. It's just that it is no longer the first thing I see whenever I pick up the phone.

Like Kisa Gotami; I had been carrying my dead son around everywhere. I was symbolically carrying my child on my left shoulder and finally; I let go of the metaphorical body I was clinging to. It was a huge turning point for me.

I also realised the pain of my left shoulder began from the day I found him dead, and I no longer have flashbacks of discovering his body. I had finally let go of that *dukkha*.

CHAPTER 14

GRIEF CAN CRIPPLE OR LIBERATE YOU

Grief is a strange thing. It can ruin us, or it can, paradoxically, be a beautiful catalyst to a liberated life. It can cut us open like a knife and leave us scarred or open us like a flower – ultimately the choice is ours!

Although grief is perfectly natural and normal, one should avoid the trap of falling into perpetual lamentation and self-pity, which only leads to unnecessary hardship and misery. For grief to be a catalyst toward a liberated life, we must avoid reinforcing the new identity as a grieving parent. When we are ready, *and only then,* we begin to gradually detach and start letting go of that persona.

When intense grief has passed, we must allow a sense of humour back into our lives and not feel guilty if we allow ourselves to laugh. If we truly understand impermanence, we will see the lighter side of things even in the grimmest situations. About a year after my son died, my friend called me a comedian when I made her break into fits of laughter about something that bothered her. It was a relief for me to make someone laugh and I recognised an important milestone in my recovery had been reached.

There is no benefit to prolonged grief

To stop misery and lamentation, one must realise that there is no benefit to prolonged grief - because no amount of grief can bring the dead back. I must accept that my beloved child has gone, and I will never see him again - I have to remind myself of this daily. Whilst I will always love and cherish him for as long as I live, I must also honour him by moving forward to find happiness and a sense of humour again. He loved me deeply and he would have dearly wanted me to be happy or to quote his words, to *'put the magic'* back into my life.

I found much wisdom reading the *suttas* on what the Buddha advised. The one that really helped me is the *Salla Sutta (The Arrow).*[72] Here the Buddha gave advice on how to deal with death in the family which was tailored for a grieving parent who was in so much misery that he was not able to eat or sleep after the death of his son and he was

---

[72] https://www.accesstoinsight.org/tipitaka/kn/snp/snp.3.08.than.html

starving.

The Buddha's words as set out below helped me understand that my son will never be seen by me again. He is gone. Lamentation, longing and sorrow will only bring more sorrow. They will undo nothing. It would be like allowing a knife that had been stuck in my heart to remain. I had to pull out that knife, however painful it might be.

> '... If a fire were to start in your house, you would extinguish it at once by any means, knowing that failing to do so would lead to the destruction of the house and everything in it. When afflicted by grief, extinguish it at once. The sooner you can do so, the less you will suffer. If you can see the way things truly are, you will also see that you have no better choice than to dispel your grief and sorrow at once...'[73]

We must understand that our child's death can never be undone and that we must live with this fact for the rest of our lives, whether we like it or not. And we may come to understand that wounds from this cut can transform ourselves to be the best version of ourselves.

Losing a child will make you question everything, including your own death. When we lose a loved one, we may feel

---

[73] *Salla Sutta- The Arrow* Sn 3.8 PTS: Sn 574-593, translated from the Pali by Thanissaro Bhikkhu.

sorry for our loss, we will miss our loved one; we may regret not saying that final goodbye. We will miss their laughter and their voice. We will cry, and lament. But what we may fail to fully realise is that for the person who dies, it is worse, in that, everyone is separated from him or her by the death.

Understanding that everything we love will be separated from us, whether we die before or after our loved ones, is a realisation that is simultaneously both the loss of innocence and the seed for the arising of liberation.

How can we, and by this - I mean everyone, be completely and truly happy knowing that we will also one day be separated from everyone and everything that matters to us? Indeed, this is such a dark thought that most of us live our lives in a manner to completely conceal this truth with worldly distractions. The path most of us choose to travel with a gusto until the bubble burst, i.e. when they meet a tragedy head-on, as I did.

By dying, my child had lost just about everything that had been important to him. He became separated from people as well as things he loved - family, friends, his guitar, his studio - everything he had worked hard for, his life's skills, his physical appearance, his body, his beautiful hair, his health, and even his breath. He died without the opportunity of saying goodbye. He was alone, no chance of turning back.

More than a year after the death of my son, I was fortunate to be in a forest monastery in North-East Thailand where I met Luang Por Ajahn Gangha, a wise old monk who many consider fully enlightened.[74]

So, I asked him: "How can we be truly happy if we come to the realisation that everything and everyone we love will eventually be separated from us?" As he only spoke in Thai, his advice came through an interpreter.

His reply was:

> *'It's a chance for us to accumulate parami (the ten perfections)[75]. He used a simile of standing at the edge of a very deep pit, several hundred metres deep. If we are unable to be in the present moment but stuck in the sorrows of the past - just thinking that our child is dead or worrying about the future, we will tremble and fall and there's only death awaiting us. If however, we understand the teachings of the Buddha, we would always be in the present moment. We will refrain from thinking*

---

[74] http://theseoultimes.com/ST/?url=/ST/db/read.php?idx=12987

[75] meaning of parami or the ten perfections are (1) generosity (dāna), (2) morality (sīla), (3) renunciation (nekhamma) (4) insight (paññā), (5) energy (viriya), (6) patience (khanti), (7) truthfulness (sacca), (8) resolution (adhiṭṭhāna), (9) loving-kindness (metta), and (10) equanimity (upekkhā).

about the past or the future. It's about right understanding'.

He then went on to say,

'You can fall or use this as a wonderful opportunity for liberation'.

I thought it was profound advice and took it to mean that when we encounter a terrible life-shattering experience; we are brought to life's cliff-edge. Stuck in sorrow and lamentation of the past or anxiety about the future will cause us to tremble and fall to the depths of despair. But if we are grounded in the present moment and gaze at the mighty vista that has been revealed, not rejecting any experience, we can use this as a wonderful opportunity to understand suffering and its causes and in the process move towards liberation.

Whilst we love our children deeply and fully, understanding the nature of impermanence, we should be prepared to let go and continue on our path alone.

Understanding the *Dhamma* is also understanding that our children have had many previous lives and their life with us is only but one of their many lives in their journey. Kahlil Gibran's poem, Children, makes this point:

'... Your children are not your children.
They are the sons and daughters of Life's
longing for itself.
They come through you but not from you.
And though they are with you, they belong not
to you...' [76]

Whether or not we are aware of it, death is, and has always been, a central fact of life. It has always been the lighthouse in the great distance in the great ocean of our lives - in *samsara*. But the lighthouse's warning is mostly ignored by both the living and the departed, until the moment one finally awakens to the perils of existence, especially when death happens unexpectedly. And we are forced to make a determined effort, with right understanding and view, to escape this cycle of clinging.

---

[76] The Prophet by Kahlil Gibran.

CHAPTER 15

DON'T CRY BECAUSE IT'S OVER, SMILE BECAUSE IT HAPPENED

Dr. Suess

Our life is a journey that begins with birth and ends with death. Once we begin, it is not a rehearsal, but for real. The problem is that the journey continues whether we are ready or not. Most of the time, we are caught up in the ups and downs of our daily schedules that we forget to step back and see the whole picture. It is only when we encounter a major life-changing event, that we stop to really question the meaning of life.

When we encounter the death of our child, we are able to view one lifetime as a complete picture. It is actually a wondrous opportunity. That is if we are prepared to move forward from grief and reflect on the precious cycle from life to death.

We realise that we have all gone through so many transitions in our lives, from our own birth, to our first day at school, to when we met our partner to the birth of our children, to each significant moment in our lives, and many in between. It's like the seasons; they keep changing - so do our lives from moment to moment.

New Norms and Transitions

People say that when your child dies, there is a new norm. But in reality, there has always been new norms at every significant transition point of our lives. The main difference is the sudden colossal nature of death, especially unexpected death.

For women, when we get our first menstruation, there is a new norm. When we first find out we are pregnant and realise that we have a growing foetus in us, there is a new norm. When we give birth, there is a new norm. It is important to note that with each new norm there had in effect been a death of our former selves. Seeing these little deaths helped me understand that even the death of a child is a natural process inherent to life.

When our children take their first step, there's another new norm in our journey through motherhood, when they say their first word, then the first day of school. Their first exam, their first relationship, their first heartache. When they leave home, and the transitions continue. Nothing remains static.

Like me, some of us may encounter the death of our child and that creates another new norm.

Our life is a journey of transitions and we can ask: *What is this journey of transitions all about?*

No one can tell us with absolute certainty. Each religion will have its own version. According to the Buddha, don't just believe what you hear. Understand it for yourself. Most of the time, we are so caught up in our everyday business that we postpone the questions of life and death to later. It's too uncomfortable and frightening to contemplate death.

When we lose a child, we have the unique opportunity to see the complete lifetime from birth to death; we will see that each lifetime is comprised of a stream of singular moments of births and deaths. The baby was not the same as the child, the child was not the same as the adolescent; and the adolescent was not the same as the adult. They were neither the same nor totally different persons.

So, it is not only at the end of our child's life that we encountered their death, but we have confronted many 'deaths' during the many transitions in their lifetime.

At any given moment, one part of our lives is already gone,

and the next is yet to happen. My son lived to the age of thirty. But my baby son had 'died' a long time ago, then again as the child, then again as the teenager, then again as the young adult and finally as a young thirty years old man when I found him dead on his bed.

I remember when my son was in his late teens, I would sometimes cry when I looked at old photos of him as a child. I did not realise then, but that was my way of grieving the change or my loss of the young child whom I had lovingly raised since I learned I was pregnant with him.

By the time he died, all his twenty-nine years of life had been 'dying' moment by moment. So, when he ultimately died, he had already died many times before.

I remember when I brought my children to kindergarten, there were some stay-home mums who cried at the school gate-sad to see their babies leave homes for school. In a way, they were grieving impermanence-the transformation of their children from babies to young children. They were also grieving the transition of their roles as full-time mothers in their own lives. A part of them had also died when their babies had transitioned to young children. As a working mother, I could not understand that, but I understand now.

When we lose someone dear to us, we cannot help but cultivate our own personal awareness of death and an appreciation of the fragility of life.

Driverless Bus

Once we are born, there's no turning back. We must continue on this journey. It's like we are on a bus where once we are on it, it's almost impossible to change the route. And later we realise that this bus does not even have a driver whom we can request a change of route. I am not saying that you can't change your situation, but that life has its own realities which have to be accepted, and it is that acceptance that gives liberation, purpose and real meaning.

We don't know exactly where we are going and when, we can only look behind and gather experiences as tools to help us in our next stop. Where the bus stops will depend on many things and whether the conditions are right for that stop. It can be a good, bad or neutral stop. Although we can't control the direction of the bus, we can control how we respond to the journey.

There are <u>always</u> choices as to how we respond to any journey, even in the most formidable circumstances. For example, in a Nazi concentration camp where everything is taken away from a person except for one thing: the last of the human freedoms to choose how one responds to a given set of circumstances. Viktor Frankl said,

> *'Every day, every hour, offered an opportunity to make a decision … whether you would become the*

plaything of circumstance, renouncing freedom and dignity to be moulded into the form of the typical inmate.'[77]

We can under any set of circumstances decide how we should respond-and exercise our last of freedoms to choose how we respond in the worse of situations that life may throw us.

---

[77] Man's Search for Meaning by Viktor Frankl.

CHAPTER 16

YOU WON'T BE THE SAME PERSON WHO WALKED IN

When you come out of the storm, you won't be the same person who walked in. That's what this storm is about – Haruki Murakami

When I was confronted with my child's death, I evaporated into an unrecognisable form of myself. I was thrown into an unfamiliar world. It was not what I imagined, not what I had ever envisaged and certainly not what I planned my life to be. I felt like an alchemical transformation had taken place except it was from gold to iron.

People told me that I was strong and that I was handling the death of my son well. But that was not true-I was weak, I was sad, and I was vulnerable, and my heart was terribly broken. It was as if a knife had cut right into my heart, ripping it apart. It felt like a terrifying free-fall, not knowing where or when I would land. The solid ground on which I stood had become mud.

I wondered and hoped there would be a way out of this mud of grief; perhaps through the power of compassion and wisdom?

When we move through the terrible transformation of loss and grief, we may discover the liberating truth of the impermanence of everything in our life. The past is like a dream–unreliable, as it is based on our coloured perceptions. The future as we may imagine it; may not happen. Grief and sorrow may teach us gratitude for what we have, even the 'gift' of the noble truth of suffering. If we can understand how to let go of grief, we may even find happiness on the other side.

Kintsugi
I came across an article about *Kintsugi* during the time I was in intense grief.

Kintsugi is a Japanese method for repairing broken ceramics with a special lacquer mixed with gold, silver, or platinum. The philosophy behind the technique is to recognise the history of the object and to visibly incorporate the repair into the new piece instead of trying to disguise it.[78]

I thought about how useful it would be to apply such a philosophy to my grief process.

My heart was broken terribly by my son's death. To give meaning to loss is not to erase the suffering but to take the whole landscape of our lives, not rejecting or denying our experiences, and to realise the truth of suffering. Like the ceramic vase of *Kintsugi*, the loss of a child can leave a mother's heart scarred and flawed, but by becoming profoundly aware of the truth of suffering that same loss can make her more courageous, compassionate and wiser.

I found that I was becoming more sensitive to others and gravitated towards helping parents who had lost a child. Having gone through such suffering myself, I was naturally gravitated to helping someone going through the same suffering.

---

[78] https://www.thisiscolossal.com/2014/05/kintsugi-the-art-of-broken-pieces/

CHAPTER 17

BE PREPARED TO LET GO OF SUFFERING

How am I to comprehend this? How am I to have it? Why am I robbed, and who is benefited? - Mark Twain

When we have children, we love them; we nourish them, we teach them well and we protect them. We hope that now and when we are old and frail, they will love us and protect us.

Mark Twain in his letter when his daughter died said:

> *'You have seen our whole voyage. You have*
> *seen us go to sea, a cloud of sail-and the flag at*
> *the peak; and you see us now, chartless, adrift-*
> *derelicts; battered, water-logged, our sails a*
> *ruck of rags, our pride gone. For it is gone. And*
> *there is nothing in its place. The vanity of life*
> *was all we had, and there is no more vanity left*
> *in us. We are even ashamed of that we had;*
> *ashamed that we trusted the promises of life*
> *and builded high-to come to this!'* [79]

Many of us take pride in the achievements of our children. When our son or daughter dies, our pride is suddenly vanished, and we may also feel ashamed. There is nothing more humbling than the death of one's child.

Mark Twain also said,

> *'To me she was but treasure in the bank; the*
> *amount known, the need to look at it daily,*
> *handle it, weigh it, count it, realise it, not*
> *necessary; and now that I would do it, it is too*
> *late; they tell me it is not there, has vanished*
> *away in a night, the bank is broken, my fortune*
> *is gone, I am a pauper.'*

---

[79] https://mark-twain.classic-literature.co.uk/mark-twains-letters-1886-1900/ebook-page-83.asp

When our child dies, it feels like our future is crushed and our dreams robbed. This is especially difficult for people who have to rely on their adult children for physical and financial support.

The Buddhist perspective on death

Ajahn Brahm summarised the Buddhist perspective well when he said,

> *'When you see none of this belongs to you, the arrows of suffering have no target'* [80].

So, whilst we love unconditionally, we must always be prepared to let go of our loved ones when the time comes; for we all have our own journeys and we must be prepared to continue on and allow ourselves to open like a flower.

As expressed by the Buddha in the *Salla Sutta*.

Salla Sutta: The Arrow[81]

'There is no means by which those who are born will not die... of those overcome by death and passing to another world, a father cannot hold back his son, nor relatives a relation... But the wise do not grieve, having realised the nature of the world. You do not know the path by which they came or departed. Not

---

[80] https://bswa.org/teaching/letting-go-of-fear-by-ajahn-brahm/

[81] Sn 3.8 PTS: Sn 574-593 Salla Sutta

seeing either end, you lament in vain. If any benefit
is gained by lamenting, the wise would do it...
Seeing a dead body, one should know, 'He will not
be met by me again.' As the fire in a burning house
is extinguished with water, so a wise, discriminating,
learned and sensible man should quickly drive away
the sorrow that arises... He who seeks happiness
should withdraw the arrow: his own lamentations,
longings and grief'.

CHAPTER 18

MESSAGES FROM BEYOND

Speaking with other grieving parents I have come to know that most parents believe they have received messages from their departed children. I am no exception, and in this chapter, I will share some of the strange occurrences which I believe were messages from my son.

For my son to have wanted to reach out would have been entirely in his character because he always believed in putting the magic into every relationship and even wrote a song of that title.

His friends remember him as the person who never forgot to make their gatherings special. He was a giving and caring person and would take the extra effort just to help someone in need.

At family Christmas parties, he would come in with a huge

bag of home-made bath soaps and candles and would hand over a gift to each and every one just to make their Christmas special.

The Scent

A few years before he died, my son bought me a jasmine plant for Mother's Day and planted it for me in the garden. The first message from him occurred seven days after he died, when I felt him next to me on my bed one morning. The smell of jasmine was very distinct, and I called out to the rest of the family to come quickly but by the time they had come the scent had unfortunately dissipated.

The Dragonfly

The second message was about ten days after he died. It was on the day we invited two of his closest friends to pick their favourite keepsake from his personal possessions. The most beautiful golden dragonfly appeared in our garden and sat on the gazebo. It stayed motionless for two hours straight. Nothing like this has ever happened in the twelve years since we have lived here. It didn't move at all while we examined it closely and photographed it. Even our dog's close proximity to it did not prompt it to fly away. Later that night, we saw it again at our back door.

We shared the love of dragonflies. He was born in the year of the dragon under the Chinese zodiac calendar. Sometime later, while going through the songs on his computer, we found the last song played by him was his own composition called 'Dragonfly'.

photo of the dragonfly by Jake

The dragonfly we saw in the garden on that day looked like a piece of golden jewellery and when I saw it, I knew that it was Brian's message to me that he was doing well. It was a significant message for me. He had lacquered boxes with a gold dragonfly painted on it.

Also, his DJ name was Khameleon, and I took this to mean that he liked to remain close but hidden from view - like an angel.

The Song

The third message came just the day after the Coroner's office informed us that there were no drugs or substances in his body. It came through the song sung by a busker at the doorstep of my place of work. I took this to be a message from my departed son for several reasons, including the fact that never before had there been a busker at my workplace, and the lyric seemed like a message from him:

> **Time of Your Life** by Greenday[82]
> 'Another turning point, a fork stuck in the road
> Time grabs you by the wrist, directs you where to
> go. So, make the best of this test and don't ask
> why. It's not a question, but a lesson learned in
> time. It's something unpredictable, but in the end
> it's right. I hope you had the time of your life'.

I have had heard this popular song many times before but the significance of it at this time was, to me, completely unmistakable.

And there were other mysteries. My son by his deeds and words seemed to expect he would have a short life. It was only after his death that my sister shared with me that when he was in his teens, he asked her *'Aunty Jessie, do you believe in fortune-tellers?'* and she said *'no'*. Then he said

---

[82] This song by Greenday is commonly played at funerals.

*'neither do I but I believe in the lines on my palm '*and added that he did not believe that he would live past thirty. He showed her the very short 'lifeline' on his palm. She then said to him, *'did you show your parents?'* and he replied, *'No, you don't tell your parents these sorts of things'*.

After his death, his friends told me that he had on several occasions told them that he believed he would have a short life. No one took this seriously. Personally, I neither believe in fortune-telling nor palmistry but I do recognise that we can become what we believe. The Buddha said that *'the mind is the forerunner of all things'*[83]. My son's belief that he had a short life may have been a factor to him dying young.

In a way, it was good that my son thought of his own death and impermanence. Many of us live as if we are going to live forever. It is only when terminal illness happens or if we know we are going to die in the near future, we change our view to life.

He lived as if every encounter with me may be our last as he would always kiss me when he saw me and end his conversations with 'I love you mum'. I am told that he was as affectionate to his friends too with hugs and loving words at every encounter with them too.

---

[83] *Dhammapada verse 1*

I am grateful for the journey with my son. He taught me by his life and death to live in the present moment and not to postpone things for later. This applies to everything we do.

CHAPTER 19

WHAT NOT TO SAY TO BEREAVED MOTHERS

Right Speech is the third factor of the Noble Eightfold Path.[84] We should strive for right speech at all times. Before saying anything, especially to people who may be grieving or vulnerable, we should always check: Is it true, is it helpful, is it kind?

Be mindful of your own fears and your own vulnerabilities when you face the grief of another mother. Too many people unfortunately just speak without mindfulness. They are not aware their own fears are often brought to surface when they face a grieving parent. So, they feel that to overcome their own vulnerability, they have to say something, anything - just to soothe their own fears. Unfortunately, being unskilled, they usually say the wrong

---

[84] https://tricycle.org/magazine/noble-eightfold-path/

things to a bereaved mother. If you have not experienced the grief of losing a child, it's better to avoid giving advice, but just say, 'I'm sorry for your loss, or, I am here for you'.

Remember, the bereaved mother is feeling so much pain, sadness, anger, guilt and isolation. Before saying think and reflect: is it going to make her feel worse?

Compassion sometimes means just being present and saying, 'I'm here for you'. It often takes a lot of courage just to sit by her and listen. If she feels that she can trust you, she will tell you, at a suitable time, how she feels.

I have listed some statements that are better left unsaid or avoided, based on my own experience as well as that of other bereaved mothers I have had conversations with:

- *'Just focus on your other children'.*

A grieving mother usually feels like a failure that she could not protect her child. To now ask her *'just to focus on her other children'* would suggest to her that she is not a good mother to her other children too. What gives anyone the right to assume that she is not properly looking after her other children, even in her grief. A mother's love is big enough for all her children.

- *God has a plan.*

To me, as a Buddhist, this seems to be a call to accept tyrannical behaviour. So even if this is your belief, be mindful to keep this to yourself. This statement may, however, be appropriate if you were saying this to someone who shares your views.

- *Any sentence that begins with 'at least' should be avoided*

Statements such as 'at least you have other children', 'at least he did not suffer, at least you were blessed to have him', would be diminishing a bereaved mother's loss. She needs to feel that her loss is validated, and not diminished.

- *I know how you feel. I have lost a parent.*

Whilst the loss of a parent is sad for the family, but it is completely different from losing a child. The intensity of the loss and the gravity of the suffering cannot and should not be compared.

- *I couldn't do what you did. You are so strong.*

People are generally not comfortable when a grieving person falls apart. So, by saying *'you are so strong'*, is likely a warning to her not to cry or fall apart in their presence. By saying this, a bereaved mother may feel that you are putting a lid on her grief. She may feel pressured to be 'strong'.

- *I can't imagine what you are going through.*

When you consider this statement carefully, you will realise that actually it *is* possible for anyone to imagine losing their precious child. So, what is really being said is 'I don't want to imagine your loss'. It is a statement about the speaker's own feelings than it is about the grieving parent's feelings. When speaking with a grieving parent try to focus on helping them through their darkest hour. You will have the time to deal with your own feelings later.

- *You should try to get over it.*

Anything that implies 'getting over it' will only add more unnecessary pain and hurt to a bereaved mother. At this time her pain should be acknowledged and not dismissed nor diminished. She will never *just* get over it, but she will hopefully move forward in time, at her own time. Don't have expectations as to how much time she needs or ought to need unless you have been through the exact same experience. And remember because there are no two identical sets of circumstances in these matters, you cannot have experienced the same thing anyway, especially if you haven't even lost a child yourself.

CHAPTER 20

IF YOU COULD GO BACK, WOULD YOU DO IT ALL AGAIN?

Death is not the greatest loss in life. The greatest loss is what dies inside us while we live' - Norman Cousins.

Losing a child brings a pain unlike any other. No one would wish this upon another, yet this grief-curse 'gift' can bring us a much deeper understanding and appreciation for all that is important.

My son has taught me that it is not how long we live but how well we live that matters.

In his short life he has touched the lives of so many and has given content and meaning to many people. Several music tributes have been done by his friends and a lovely song has been written about him[85]. He has inspired me to write this book to help others in their journey.

He has been my son, friend, teacher, and in some ways like a father. I have learnt so much from him. I have learned to express love more openly, to hug loved ones whenever I see them and to give them a kiss on the cheek when they leave.

I have learned to live for the moment from his simple words *'if not now then, when mum?'*, and not to take anything or anyone for granted. I now fully understand and can say with certainty that nothing is certain or within our control.

My son's death has taught me the great danger of life, and at the same time, how to live a meaningful and happier life. So simple but yet so profound. He has taught me to see the profoundness in the simplicity of life's truths.

As expressed by Viktor Frankl:

> *'the meaning of life differs from person to person, from day to day and from hour to hour.'*

And:

> *'what matters, therefore is not the meaning of life in general but rather the specific meaning of a*

---

[85] *'When your lights are low'* by Skyuka, available on iTunes

> person's life at a given moment'. One should not
> search for an abstract meaning of life. It varies from
> situation to situation and is not stagnant. There is
> no one meaning for all. We can find meaning in life
> even in a hopeless situation'

And he said:

> 'Human potential at its best is to transform a
> personal tragedy into a triumph, to turn one's
> predicament into a human achievement'.

To me when my child died, I had to find a new meaning to my life. I started writing and continued writing every day and sometimes all day. I took time off work just to resolve all the emotions I was going through. It was cathartic, and I kept crying as I wrote each paragraph. I must have cried a million tears as I wrote my journal.

I would advise anyone who has gone through a tragic loss to write a journal on a daily basis to help understand the loss and the grieving.

Writing also allowed me to review the whole landscape of my journey with my son, not rejecting or denying what has been thrust upon me. It has helped me appreciate and be grateful for the thirty wonderful years we had together. This has made me gain a better understanding of why we are on this journey called life.

The meaning of life is to end suffering. We are given many curved balls in life - it is how we react at any given situation that matters - to be the best version of ourselves.

I have now understood these *painful truths*:

- Fear and worry about death are just wasted energy. Whenever I feel anxious and start worrying about the safety of my loved ones, I visualise my son, dead at home on his own bed where he was supposed to be safest and I instantly realise that fear, and worry are useless;

- The universal truth that life is impermanent, and nothing is to be taken for granted;

- Our children can die before us;

- The death of our child changes our whole perspective to life; there is nothing more humbling than to suffer the loss of a child;

- There is nothing we can do to bring our loved ones back, not even offering ourselves in their place;

- Forgiveness, especially for ourselves that our child is dead, and we are still alive, is one of the hardest things to do;

- We have no control as to what happens to us, but we

have the freedom to choose whether to be a victim or the survivor of the loss;

- We will never get over the death of our child, but we can move forward, and we can laugh again even while the truth that we are all born to die;

- Life promises nothing. It's a precious opportunity to learn and grow from whatever comes your way;

- Believing we are in control is a delusion;

- No one, no pill can stop the suffering – we alone must walk the path to recovery and wisdom;

- We can never have enough time with our children, even a hundred years is not enough;

- Moving forward means accepting that the death can never be undone, and that we must be prepared to let go of the grief;

- The small things like a hug, a smile, and a call just to say you care are the important things in life;

- Unless we can avoid attachment, we can never avoid grief.

'Everything will be okay in the end, and if it's not okay, it's not the end'[86].

As a Buddhist with *nibbana* as my ultimate goal, the purpose of my life is to understand 'suffering' at its root. This will lead to that final liberation.

---

[86] John Lennon

LYRICS

Opens Like a Flower, Cut it with a Knife

Brian Nikhil Mitra

Opens like a flower
Cut it with a knife.
Slowly pouring down
Going to let it out now

Rivers pouring down from the sky
Drowning all the people who did not get to the high
People watch the tides ride.
Cos you are not alone.

Unravelling, absolutely everything
Slowly pouring down
I'm gonna let it all out now

Rivers pouring out of my eyes
Numbing all my sorrows down

With a pipe and a sigh
People watch your love die
We are not alone.

Unravelling, absolutely everything
Slowly pouring down
I'm gonna let it all out now
Are you ready?

Opens like a Flower, cut it with a knife
Slowly pouring down
I'm gonna let it all out now

Opens like a Flower, cut it with a knife
This is it.
Is it all of it?
Is it just like we planned?

If you could go back, would you do it all again?
If you could go back, would you do it all again?

MY EULOGY

Brian, my son, my love, my life. Today I must say my final good bye to your body.

Thank-you for choosing me to be your mum, to give birth to you and to help nurture you. But you had your own character and personality which you brought with you.

I always knew that our journey together would end but hoped that I would go first. A mother's attachment to her only son is so great that the very thought of losing him is so unbearable that she would do everything in her power to protect him from harm from the time he is born. The hardest thing in my life was to open the door to find you dead on your bed that morning. I would have gladly and without hesitation given my life to protect you from harm. My heartache and pain will continue for a long, long time and maybe for this whole lifetime.

The Buddha taught the four noble truths. The first truth is that life is suffering. Suffering-a truth that is hard to imagine when there is so much happiness and fun most of the time.

Then seeing you dead on the bed, seeing your beautiful face and body just lying there motionless and there was nothing I could do to help you, my darling son, I deeply understood the meaning of suffering. The cruel and painful suffering of separation. The fragility and impermanence of life and the fact that we can't control anything.

The dharma has helped me through this difficult time and will continue to help me to make sense of it all. There is no guarantee about anything in this world except that with birth comes death at any time and often when least expected.

Brian, our journey although short has enriched me in more ways that can be imagined.

You taught me patience, humility, love and gentleness. You taught me that it is ok to be good just for goodness sake.

You always showed me affection and love. You were the most gentle, compassionate and loving being I have ever known. You taught me to listen not just by what was said but with my heart and mind. You loved your family unconditionally and would do anything to protect us.

Brian and I had a very loving relationship. He would always hug me whenever he saw me and hug me when he left with a kiss on my cheek. Even if he saw me more than once that day, he would do the same. At the end of every phone call especially in our later years together, he would always end with "love you". I was very touched when I saw the words on your studio wall. LOVE IS? in and next to it was written my mum. Although it was on your studio, I only noticed yesterday this when I watched the video. In your death, you were are also reminding me that you loved me unconditionally. How beautiful to have been loved by you so much.

Brian had a deep understanding of life as can be seen in the songs he wrote, and from the numerous tributes from people whose lives he touched. Tonight from 11pm to 1am there will be two- hour techno music tribute to Brian by radio RTRFM.

Brian was a free- sprit and a non-conformist and was often misunderstood for just being himself.

Brian found it difficult to follow rules and even as young as four when I brought him to music school – I remember all the children were seated facing the teacher ... all except one ...Brian who would sit facing the children and this happened at almost every lesson. He would get in trouble for this but couldn't understand what he was doing wrong.

In his school days, he would sometimes get into trouble for his free spirit. Asking too many questions. I also remember once in Religions Education class in Aquinas college, we were called up because Brian was using a fake set of teeth and was making the boys laugh.

Brian was very intelligent but because he had ADHD, he had difficulty concentrating and was sometimes frustrated because he was misunderstood.

These last few days have been extremely difficult for Jake, Nicole, Mona and myself and I know many of you here today.

During the past few days, my strength has come from Jake, Nicole and Mona, our extended families, the Sangha, friends and also reading all the Facebook tributes. Knowing that he has touched the hearts of so... so many has helped ease my pain. Although I knew that Brian was kind, gentle and loving, I had no idea of the magnitude of his kindness.

His friends have been telling that Brian was always there for them. His music studio was not just a place of business but a meeting place for many who just needed sometime from the busy world. I am told - a place they could come to talk after a hard day knowing that Brian would listen without judging.

Brian has shown by his action that ultimately only kindness and love matters.

METTA SUTTA

This is what should be done
By one who is skilled in goodness,
And who knows the path of peace:
Let them be able and upright,
Straight forward and gentle in speech.
Humble and not conceited,
Contented and easily satisfied.
Not busy with duties and frugal in their ways.
Peaceful and calm, and wise and skillful,
Not proud and demanding in nature.
Let them not do the slightest thing
That the wise would later reprove.
Wishing: In gladness and in safety,
May all beings be at ease.
Whatever living beings there may be;
Whether they are weak or strong, omitting none,
The great or the mighty, medium, short or small,
The seen and the unseen,
Those living near and far away,
Those born and to-be-born,
May all beings be happy,
Let none deceive another,
Or despise any being in any state.
Let none through anger or ill-will

Wish harm upon another.
Even as a mother protects with her life
Her child, her only child,
So with a boundless heart
Should one cherish all living beings:
Radiating kindness over the entire world
Spreading upwards to the skies,
And downwards to the depths;
Outwards and unbounded,
Freed from hatred and ill-will.
Whether standing or walking, seated or lying down
Free from drowsiness,
One should sustain this recollection.
This is said to be the sublime abiding.
By not holding to false views,
The pure-hearted one, having clarity of vision,
Being freed from all sense desires is not born again
into this world.[87]

[87] Translation by Ajahn Brahm

ABBREVIATIONS

AN   *Anguttara Nikaya*

DN   *Digha Nikaya*

DP   *Dhammapada*

MN   *Majjhima Nikaya*

SN   *Samyutta Nikaya*

Vin   *Vinaya*

GLOSSARY

Ajahn
Teacher of more than ten years of monastic life (Thai)

anapanasati
Mindfulness of breathing.

anatta
Not-self. anicca Impermanence or uncertainty.

anicca-dukkha-anatta
The three characteristics of existence: impermanence, suffering, and not-self.

arahant
One who has reached the highest state of enlightenment.

bhikkhu
Buddhist monk.

Buddha
"One who knows"; one who is awakened, who represents the state of enlightenment or awakening.

dhamma
The teachings of the Buddha

dukkha
First Noble Truths: Suffering: un-satisfactoriness; the inherent imperfection of conditioned phenomena.

Eightfold Path
Eight factors of spiritual practice leading to the extinction of suffering: Right View (or Right Understanding), Right Thought (Right Intention), Right Speech, Right Action, Right Livelihood, Right Effort, Right Mindfulness, Right Concentration.

Five Precepts
The five basic guidelines for training oneself in wholesome actions of body and speech: refraining from killing other beings; refraining from stealing; responsible sexual conduct; refraining from lying and false speech; refraining from the use of intoxicants.

the five khandas
form; feeling; perception; mental formations and the sense consciousnesses.

kusala
Wholesome or skillful actions or mental states.

Luang Por
Venerable Father, Respected Father; a friendly and reverential term of address used for elderly monks.

magga
Path. See Eightfold Path.

Maha
Title given to monks who have studied Pali and completed up to the fourth year or higher.

Mara
Evil and temptation personified; a powerful malevolent deity ruling over the highest heaven of the sensual sphere; personification of the defilements, the totality of worldly existence, and death.

metta
Loving-kindness.

nāma
Nonmaterial (mental) phenomena (Also: nāma-dhamma).

nanadassana
Knowledge and insight (into the Four Noble truth

nibbana
The state of liberation from all suffering and defilements,
the goal of the Buddhist path (Sanskrit: nirvana).

nibbida
Disenchantment or disinterest in fires or passions of the
sensual world.

Path
Eightfold Path.

paticcasamuppada
Conditioned arising, dependent origination; one of the
central doctrines of the Buddhist teaching.

piti
Rapture; the third factor of absorption.

rupa
Material or physical objects, corporeality

samadhi
Concentration, one-pointedness of mind, mental stability;
state of concentrated calm resulting from meditation
practice.

samana
A religious seeker living a renunciant life. Originating from

the Sanskrit term for

samsara
Wheel of Existence; "perpetual wandering"; the continuous process of being born, growing old, suffering, and dying again and again; the world of all conditioned phenomena, mental and material.

Siddhatta Gotama
The original name of the historical Buddha.

sila
Virtuous conduct or morality.

sukka
Happiness or contentment.

sutta
A discourse of the Buddha as recorded in the Pali canon (Sanskrit word is sutra).

Tanha
Craving or desires conditioned by greed, hatred and ignorance and is the cause of dukkha in the cycles rebirth.

Tipitaka
The Buddhist canon. (Sanskrit: Tripiṭaka.)

upekkha
Equanimity.

upadana
Grasping, clinging, attachment

vinaya
The Buddhist monastic code of discipline

worldly dramas
The eight worldly conditions of gain and loss, praise and blame, happiness and suffering, fame and disrepute.

REFERENCES

Man's Search for Meaning: Frankl, V.

When the Bough Breaks: Judith R. Bernstein

Broken Open: Elizabeth Lessder

Bearing the Unbearable: Joanne Cacciatorre

Beyond Tears: Ellen Mitchell

Its Ok not to be Ok: Meghan Devine

When Bad things happen to Good People: Harold Kushner

Shattered: Rebecca Tervo

No Death No Fear: Thich Nhat Hanh

On Grief and Grieving: David Kessler, Elizabeth Kubler-Ross

The Prophet: Kahlil Gibran

A Grief Observed: C.S. Lewis

Grieving Mindfully: Sameet Kumar

A Buddhist Journey Observed: Guy Newman

Mindfulness Bliss and Beyond: Ajahn Brahm

Opening the Door of Your Heart: Ajahn Brahm

Falling is Flying: Ajahn Brahm and Chan Master Guojun

Sutta Central: Bhante Sujato

Making friends With Death: Judith L Leith

The Art of Happiness: The Dalai Lama

When Things Fall Apart: Pema Chodron

The Wise Hearth: Jack Kornfield

Food for the heart: Jack Kornfield

The Wise Heart: Jack Kornfield

Standing at the Edge: Joan Halifax

All About Buddhism: S Dhammika

Letting Go of the Person You used to be: Lama Surya

ACKNOWLEDGEMENTS

I am deeply grateful to the many wonderful people, especially my family, relatives and friends for their love and support during my difficult journey. It is not possible to mention everyone by name, but there are a few people I would like to mention. My husband, Jake, who has been my rock, for his unconditional love and support. His gift of the Dhamma to me many years ago. I express my deep gratitude to Jake for his significant contribution to this book.

Nicole and Mona, our daughters and best friends who have been my light and joy and have done their very best to take care of me during the difficult times, even though they themselves were suffering the loss of their only brother. They have also supported me in the book. David Jones, my soon to be son-in-law who did the audio recording of the book.

Thanks also to those who helped me in various ways, with

the book, especially, Ava for her comments, Boon Tan for the sketch of the lotus on the cover, Andy, Julie, Lay Har and Manel. My gratitude also to the bereaved mothers who have become my friends in this journey and who have shared their stories with me.

I would also like to express my gratitude and appreciation to my dhamma teachers and friends, especially to Ajahn Brahmmavamso Maha Thera (Ajahn Brahm), who has been my mentor and teacher for more than twenty years. Also, to Ajahn Brahmali, for perusing the book on the relevance of the suttas.

Most importantly, I would like to thank my dear son, Brian Nikhil Mitra for his thirty-year journey with me, for which I am eternally grateful. I also thank him for his song and for helping me understand this arduous journey called life.

ABOUT THE AUTHOR

Shortly after graduating from the National University of Singapore, Cecilia Mitra was offered a partnership in a legal firm. She subsequently started her own legal practice.

In 1996, she migrated to Australia with her husband and three children. She then obtained a master's degree from the University of Western Australia while working as a lecturer. Cecilia was then offered a doctoral scholarship but decided not to pursue academia. She joined her husband's business in the dental industry in 2000.

After her children completed school, she served as a

volunteer on several organisations. This included the role of president of The Buddhist Society of Western Australia from 2013 to 2015.

In 2015, she organised the 9th Global Conference on Buddhism - Resolving Conflict with Mindfulness. This event attracted 900 delegates from around the world and featured 20 international speakers. Also, in 2015, Cecilia was instrumental in resolving a visa legislation issue for Buddhist monastics on *vows of poverty*, which led to a change in the law.

From 2016 to 2019, Cecilia held the position of president of the Federation of Australian Buddhist Councils. In this role, she was involved in the formulation of parliamentary, senate inquiry and other positional statements. This included meetings in the Federal Parliament, and at the Prime Minister's Office.

Cecilia also serves as an Honorary Secretary on the International Buddhist Confederation.

She teaches meditation and serves voluntarily on the Human Research Ethics Committee of the South Metropolitan Hospitals, Western Australia.